MW01222220

1,037 *WAYS*
TO MAKE
OR SAVE UP TO
$100,000
THIS YEAR ALONE

1,037 WAYS

TO MAKE
OR SAVE UP TO
$100,000
THIS YEAR ALONE

Edward F. Mrkvicka

Instant Improvement, Inc.

Instant Improvement, Inc.
210 East 86th Street
New York, NY, 10028

Published in the United States of America

Library of Congress Catalog Card Number: 91-58260

ISBN 0-941683-16-8

Other Books By The Same Author:

THE BANK BOOK: How to Revoke Your Bank's "License to Steal" (Harper & Row)

THE RATIONAL INVESTOR (Probus Publishing)

MOVING UP (William Morrow)

BATTLE YOUR BANK — AND WIN! (William Morrow)

Co-author of:

THE COMPLETE BOOK OF PERSONAL FINANCE (Boardroom Books)

DEDICATION

This book is dedicated to Mrs. Ruth C. Mrkvicka.

ACKNOWLEDGEMENTS

I would like to thank the entire staff of our newsletter *MONEY INSIDER* for their help and dedication, which culminated in this book becoming a reality.

CONTENTS

INTRODUCTION

The average person or family is more aware of their finances than ever before. That's good, they should be. However, as my consulting experience has unfortunately proven, the focus of their interest is too often misplaced. Too many people spend most of their time and effort worrying about their investments, as opposed to focusing on their overall finances.

Financial success is an endeavor that encompasses virtually every daily transaction. Why should a dollar spent at the grocery store receive less thought than a dollar you invest in the stock market? Yet, judging from the attitude of most, the former is somehow less valuable than the latter. That's a huge mistake. You should count every dollar because every dollar counts.

Many people have a broker — an investment adviser — they try and get the highest interest on their savings account, and so on. Then they buy whatever insurance their insurance salesman tells them they need. They buy a used car that's going to fall apart in a few hundred miles because they didn't know what to look for when making the purchase — or they hire a remodeling contractor for a home improvement and sign his boilerplate contract that does anything but adequately protect their property. The point being, on the subject of personal finance, unless you're a millionaire who has more money invested than you could possibly spend in a year, most are penny wise and dollar foolish.

What good is making a high return on your savings if you turn around and give it and more away by signing a bad car lease agreement? What good is making an excellent purchase of a growing stock if the profit is, in effect, lost because you made an error in purchasing excessively costly health insurance? The bottomline is this: your financial efforts,

11

which probably have been directed to investments, will fare far better if you take an equal amount of time to learn the thousands of ways you can make and save money in areas you are probably ignoring.

Investments are important, and I review the subject, albeit from a differing perspective, later. But, for most, the real crux of their finances is in those everyday transactions where they're getting beat, and beat badly, without even being aware they lost money. Does it really matter if you make $1,000 in extra saving's interest or save $1,000 in negotiating a loan? Of course not. Because of the nature of those returns, the savings, which would have been forever lost, and therefore subsequently unproductive, can now be expanded by being utilized by your investment program. Which is why it can be argued that savings are even more important than earnings.

Every section of this book was written because of its import to total financial maintenance. Some, while perhaps appearing to be something one might use but once in a lifetime (a will for example), are included because I know that a mistake could be ruinous.

In this book, you'll find more than 1,000 ways to make and save thousands — even 100,000 — of dollars. The secrets of success I'll share with you don't require complicated formulas or special knowledge. They are exciting, easy-to-use strategies that absolutely anyone can use — starting today.

You can read this book in order, or start with any section that particularly interests you. Whatever you choose, I think you'll find that, by following the simple steps I've outlined on the following pages, you can start making and saving money in ways you never dreamed possible.

SECRETS, TIPS, & TACTICS

A NEW PERSPECTIVE

One of the hardest aspects of my financial consulting is to get clients to understand that most traditional thinking is detrimental to their money wellbeing. Traditional thinking is the thought process that causes borrowers to immediately run to their local bank for a mortgage when, in most instances, that should be their last stop. Usually, far better terms can be garnered from private mortgage sources than from a bank, but we have been conditioned to follow certain costly paths in our financial lives. Those who understand the importance of their finances have learned that it pays to find alternatives to acquire what they need.

A most important facet of non-traditional financial thinking is realizing that it's not just the money you may have lost in a transaction that's important, but the loss of the use of the money from that point forward. Once that is understood, it is easy to see why it's required to spend time and effort on every exchange. For example, if you are paying $10.00 a month for a service you don't need, how much money are you losing over a five year period? Ten, twenty, thirty years? Most people would say the cost for five years is $600.00 ($10 x 60 months). That's true if the question was how much did you spend? But the question was how much did you lose? To see the entire transaction you have to add the loss of the use of the money wasted. From the monthly chart on the next page you can see that the true loss was $773.55 — $600.00 plus interest. (The charts use a 10% interest rate compounded monthly as a fair representation of most market conditions. This is a conservative percentage as I would hope that your investments return more than 10%.) Take this example to the thirty year mark to make the loss of the use of money even more obvious. Established thinking

states our example would lose $3,600.00 over thirty years
($10.00 x 360 months), but if, instead of being careless with
that money, you invested it as a $10.00 a month payment to
an investment program you would have a thirty year account balance of $22,412.91. Again, traditional thinking says
you lost $3,600.00 — nontraditional thinking says you lost
over six times that. The real cost extrapolates to $62.26 per
month $22,412.91 divided by 360 months). Suddenly that
$10.00 a month seems worthy of consideration.

MONTHLY PAYMENTS
10% INTEREST COMPOUNDED MONTHLY

PAYMENT AMOUNT	5 YEARS	10 YEARS	20 YEARS	30 YEARS
$5	$386.78	$1,021.88	$3,777.21	$11,206.45
10	773.55	2,043.76	7,554.41	22,412.91
15	1,160.33	3,065.65	11,331.62	33,619.36
20	1,547.11	4,087.53	15,108.83	44,825.82
25	1,933.88	5,109.41	18,886.03	56,032.27
30	2,320.66	6,131.29	22,663.24	67,238.72
35	2,707.43	7,153.17	26,440.44	78,445.18
40	3,094.21	8,175.05	30,217.65	89,651.63
45	3,480.99	9,196.94	33,994.86	100,858.08
50	3,867.76	10,218.82	37,772.06	112,064.54
Each additional $1	77.36	204.38	755.44	2,241.29

Use the monthly chart for all your expenses. While not
every dollar can or necessarily should be accounted for in
this manner, it will give you a sense of profitable perspective, as once you start seeing the total transaction, you'll be
mindful of amounts of money that previously appeared too
small to warrant concern. Not seeing the total transaction is,
unfortunately, a universal trait of the less affluent.

There are times where a loss of money occurs in a lump
sum. For example, if you failed to negotiate the closing costs

on your home mortgage, therefore paying $2,000.00 more than necessary. Traditional thinking says you lost $2,000.00. Nonsense, if you were willing to pay yourself the negotiated savings. How much does a $2,000.00 lump sum investment earn over the life of a thirty year mortgage? As you can see from the second chart, the real gain possible for you, if the money had been put to better use, is $39,205.43.

ONE TIME LUMP SUM AMOUNT
10% INTEREST COMPOUNDED MONTHLY

PAYMENT AMOUNT	5 YEARS	10 YEARS	20 YEARS	30 YEARS
$100	$164.20	$269.63	$727.02	$1,960.27
500	821.02	1,348.16	3,635.08	9,801.36
1,000	1,642.05	2,696.32	7,270.16	19,602.71
1,500	2,463.07	4,044.49	10,905.24	29,404.07
2,000	3,284.10	5,392.65	14,540.33	39,205.43
2,500	4,105.12	6,740.81	18,175.41	49,006.78
3,000	4,926.15	8,088.97	21,810.49	58,808.14
3,500	5,747.17	9,437.13	25,445.57	68,609.50
4,000	6,568.19	10,785.30	29,080.65	78,410.85
4,500	7,389.22	12,133.46	32,715.73	88,212.21
5,000	8,210.24	13,481.62	36,350.81	98,013.57
Each Additional $1	1.64	2.70	7.27	19.60

In some cases you have to combine the charts to find the total loss. For example, if you paid too much for a new car and its financing, you have to calculate the cost of the lump sum purchase loss and add it to the amount lost on the monthly installments.

To use the charts correctly, take into account, on a lump sum amount, remaining financial life; i.e., the years until retirement. Obviously, if you're forty-five, you should look at the twenty year line. While not all-inclusive for every year,

the charts give a close approximation for those years that
fall in between. The monthly chart should correspond to the
term of the loan or length of service charge. In the case of a
car loan, that may only be sixty months or less. For a continual loss, like a phone service you don't need, the time consideration may go to thirty years or beyond.

Most importantly, the charts will help you see the entire
transaction when you overpay or settle for a deal that could
have been negotiated in your favor. Consider the following
for every financial transaction:

1. GIVE EACH YOUR TIME AND EFFORT. As the
charts make clear, no amount is too small.

2. STOP DOING WHAT EVERYONE ELSE IS DOING.
On the subject of their finances, most people are unques-
tionably wrong — or they would be rich. Most so-called experts are wrong too — if that weren't the case, all their
clients would be rich, and we know they're not.

3. EXPLORE EVERY NON-TRADITIONAL MEANS
TO YOUR END. Stop immediately running to the bank with
your loan needs. Stop financing your car through the dealer.
Stop relying on your insurance agent to determine your insurance needs. Start questioning your accountant. Stop being abused by your attorney. Start demanding results from
your broker, and so on. There are other, less expensive ways
to accomplish the same tasks and goals.

4. BE CREATIVE. Limited thinking produces limited
results. I always advise clients, whether they're buying va-
cant land, selling a business, or whatever: if you can conceive
it, chances are it can be accomplished.

5. UNDERSTAND THE BETTER USE OF MONEY
CONCEPT. Again, it's not only what you make or save, but
what you do with the money from that point forward. The
better use of money is critical to financial success (and is a
theme throughout the book). Financial institutions know
that — so should every family.

Most people get beat in the majority of their financial dealings. The few who don't, usually stop there, take their money and run. The wealthy take their savings/money and apply it to other opportunities that maximize their winnings.

SAVING

To most, saving isn't one of the most stimulating topics. But that's because the public has an erroneous understanding of the concept; i.e., the word *saving* brings to mind the picture of a savings passbook at the local financial institution. In that context, saving is hard to get excited about.

I would like you to consider another definition. That is, saving is a systematic program, based on a percentage of one's salary, used for the purpose of acquiring additional wealth through various investment vehicles. Meaning, while you can use your local bank if you choose, that is not the criteria of a savings plan. Saving can be associated with any non-speculative investment, such as rare investment grade coins, mutual funds, or real estate. It's not the vehicle that determines if you're saving, it's the continuum of putting aside monies on a predetermined basis.

Let's review specifics that will clarify the advantage of saving and its ability to perform as a financial-breeder-reactor. Remember, when the word saving is used, envision whatever investment vehicle you want. In the upcoming charts we use a 10% return, which is conservative; the investment vehicle(s) you use should have a better historical return. Don't get confused if your investments don't pay interest per se, as that's not an issue. I use the term in a generic sense.

Too many of us have little or no liquid assets. This is a reflection of the fact that few of us have a savings plan. Saving money is not easy. Especially now, when many have to spend every dollar just to make ends meet. No, it's not easy, but it's mandatory for financial success.

Many years ago, saving was something everyone did. Our elders knew that if they didn't save they would be at the mercy of an uncertain future. With some money in reserve, they believed they could ride through or around rough times. History judges them correct. Sadly, with double-digit inflation and the institution of the I-want-it-now generation, saving in America declined. We have the lowest savings ratio of any industrialized nation. Saving has been replaced with things we cannot afford and in most cases don't need. People who save are often ridiculed by the so-called financial experts, who are almost unanimous in the opinion that old fashioned saving is a waste of time. They're mistaken. However, in fairness, one cannot argue that during times of record inflation, coupled with normal bank savings rates, financial institution saving is a bad investment. But that's confusing the principle. Their opinions are based on vehicle as opposed to dedication, which is where they go wrong.

For perspective, let's review bank savings which, under most market conditions, are perhaps the worst vehicle. Those who use this method at least retain a portion of what they earn. Can the same be said for those who spend, spend, spend, borrow, borrow, borrow? No, probably not, especially in light of the fact that most in the latter category usually borrow for the wrong reason. They go into debt for depreciating assets. The wealthy, or those who soon will be wealthy, only borrow for appreciating assets. The point is, even though I don't recommend saving in the traditional understanding of the word, those who do so fare better than those who don't save anything.

Again, I caution that saving, and the dedication it requires, is hard work. It takes time. You can't make a million overnight, but you can make a million. It works because of a number of factors, the most important being the effect of accumulating numbers. That is the key to any successful saving's plan. To see how it works, try this quiz. Imagine you are offered a thirty-day summer job. The manager tells you the company has alternative pay schedules. They will pay you $100,000.00 per day, or a salary that starts out at $.01 and doubles each day. On the second day you will be paid $.02, the third day $.04, and so on. Remember, this job only lasts thirty days. You have ten seconds to choose.

I've done this test with hundreds of people — most choose the $100,000.00 per day, as they quickly realize the total salary for the thirty days would be three million dollars. Three million isn't bad, but could they have done better? Let's extrapolate the doubling penny salary: 1) $.01. 2) .02. 3) .04. 4) .08. 5) .16. 6) .32. 7) .64. 8) 1.28. 9) 2.56. 10) 5.12. 11) 10.24. 12) 20.48. 13) 40.96. 14) 81.92. 15) 163.84. At the end of 15 days it appears those who chose the $100,000.00 per day were rather smart. At this juncture they have made $1,500,000.00. Those who opted for the doubling salary have made a total of only $327.67. Is it possible to catch up? 16) 327.68. 17) 655.36. 18) 1,310.72. 19) 2,621.44. 20) 5,242.88. 21) 10,485.76. 22) 20,971.52. 23) 41,943.04. 24) 83,886.08. 25) 167,772.16. 26) 335,544.32. Only four days left and we still have a problem. I say we, because I took the doubling salary, too. At this point our group has earned $671,088.63. The daily salary group has made $2,600,000.00. We're down almost two million dollars. Now its our turn. 27) 671,088.64. 28) 1,342,177.28. 29) 2,684,354.56. 30) 5,368,709.12. Total = $10,737,418.23.

Those who understand the principle of accumulating numbers, and therefore took the starting salary of a penny, achieved the best result. Those looking for a quick kill made a mistake worth the difference between the salaries, or $7,737,418.23. This example is the basis of much of what will be said from this point forward.

It may take years for a savings plan to start to add up, but, once it does, it does so rapidly, because, in addition to your added deposits, you start earning interest on interest, dividends on dividends, appreciation on appreciation, sales profit on sales profit.

The best way to illustrate this point is with a savings progression chart. But, first I have to state my Golden Rule of Saving: you must save a minimum of 5% of your gross salary every month. Now on to the charts. To further elaborate the principle of saving as a means to financial independence, I have included a 5% savings chart and a chart for the same gross salaries using a 10% figure for the more ambitious.

5% SAVINGS (10% INTEREST)

Salary	Monthly Savings	10 Years	20 Years	30 Years
$20,000	$83.33	$17,069.73	$63,278.21	$188,366.46
25,000	104.17	21,337.68	79,099.66	235,463.72
30,000	125.00	25,605.62	94,921.11	282,560.98
35,000	145.83	29,872.54	110,738.76	329,646.94
40,000	166.67	34,140.49	126,560.20	376,744.21
45,000	187.50	38,408.44	142,381.65	423,841.42
50,000	208.33	42,675.35	158,199.30	470,927.43

10% SAVINGS (10% INTEREST)

Salary	Monthly Savings	10 Years	20 Years	30 Years
$20,000	$166.66	$34,139.46	$126,566.41	$376,732.91
25,000	208.33	42,675.35	158,199.31	470,927.44
30,000	250.00	51,211.24	189,842.21	565,121.97
35,000	291.66	59,745.08	221,477.51	659,293.89
40,000	333.33	68,280.97	253,120.41	753,488.42
45,000	375.00	76,816.87	284,763.31	847,682.95
50,000	416.66	85,350.71	316,398.61	941,854.87

I hope you found the charts interesting. Like our quiz, the charts show that money accumulates at fantastic rates. It doesn't double like the salary in our example, but it does get terribly interesting between the ten and twenty year mark. That's when the effect of earning interest on interest starts to take effect. For example, look at the 10% chart on the salary line of $30,000. After ten years you have a balance of $51,211.24. During that time, you deposited $30,000.00, which means your interest was $21,211.24. At the twenty year mark you have a balance of $189,842.21. During that time, you paid a total of $60,000.00, which means your interest was a whopping $129,842.21. During that time, your accumulated interest equals more than

TWICE your deposits. Carry this line to the thirty year mark and the numbers become even more amazing. $90,000 in deposits gives $565,121.97. Such is the effect of compound interest.

There are other important considerations. One of the raps against saving is that taxes and inflation eat up a goodly portion of the return. That's true, but on balance it could be asked rhetorically, if you don't save, will you have more or less than those who do, taxes and inflation notwithstanding?

The best part is that it's inflation proof. Almost everyone receives a raise that at least equals the inflation rate, and since your monthly saving amount is a percentage of your salary, your savings plan is adjusted for inflation.

In the charts, I use specific dollar amounts to demonstrate how our principle, as expressed by my Golden Rule of Saving, can take a relatively small amount of money and expand it substantially. In actual practice, your savings plan should far exceed my figures, because your salary will increase and therefore so will the amount you save monthly; i.e., you may start out at $20,000 per year and end up at $100,000. By using a percentage, you are constantly upgrading your plan to reflect your financial status. That too is an important feature.

Saving offers other interesting possibilities.

SECOND INCOME

Salary	10 Years	20 Years	30 Years
$6,000 yr. (500 mo.)	$102,422.49	$379,684.41	$1,130,243.80
12,000 yr. (1,000 mo.)	204,844.98	759,368.82	2,260,487.90
18,000 yr. (1,500 mo.)	307,267.46	1,139,053.20	3,390,731.80

You see, if your spouse was able to work for ten years earning $12,000 per, you would have a balance, by saving it all, of \$204,844.98. If you invested that balance in a vehicle that, for example, returned twelve percent, you would have a monthly interest income of \$2,048.45 or \$24,581.40 per year. Not bad — you earned \$12,000 a year for ten years and in return you receive a yearly income of \$24,581.40 for life without ever touching the balance of \$204,844.98.

Remember, saving is a principle. What you invest in, while important from a rate perspective, isn't the point. You can save via an institutional savings plan, a mutual fund, real estate, or any other vehicle with a reasonably stable record. Your return can be achieved through interest, dividends, appreciation, sales profit, or a combination. Regardless, what makes the magic work is a dedication to the concept. Remember our summer job quiz — don't make a million dollar mistake.

THE TOP 9 MOST SECRET KEYS TO WEALTH

How do rich people acquire wealth? And once they do, how do they keep it? You'll find the answer(s) to these questions quite surprising.

First, for the purpose of this report, I am excluding those who have family wealth. The how and why in their case is inheritance, and isn't much help to the rest of us. My intention is to give you some answers that you can use in your everyday financial reality.

The remaining affluent, according to recent surveys, see themselves as hard working, industrious types who believe strongly in what might be called traditional American family values. In these days of the yuppie-millionaire, it is comforting to realize that most rich people got theirs the old fashioned way — they earned it. The hard workers still have theirs, most Wall Street yuppies don't.

This quick background sets the stage for the secrets my research has revealed. It is logical, financial bottomline thinking. And, it works.

1. IF YOU WANT TO GET WEALTHY, START YOUR OWN BUSINESS. Roughly 70% of all millionaires are self-employed or have their own company. Those kinds of statistics are hard to ignore. The old adage, "You'll never get rich working for someone else," appears to be true.

Of course, it's not quite that simple. A number of present-day millionaires previously had at least one business fail and/or they have declared personal bankruptcy. Actually, that shouldn't be discouraging. Rather, it should give you incentive to realize that no matter the outcome of your first, second, or third attempt, you still can succeed.

2. PAY YOURSELF BEFORE YOU PAY OTHERS. Regardless of where your income originates, you should take a predetermined amount from each paycheck and use it for investment purposes. Pay yourself first! If you're last in line, you'll never get paid and your investments will be non-existent.

This rule of thumb is perhaps most important of all the secrets I uncovered. Why? Because it makes everything else happen. It can finance your own business. It can give you risk capital to make investments, and so on.

Affluent people, the millionaires, recommend saving 20 to 25% of your net. You might ask how that's possible. My research indicates that a portion of the millionaires, long before they reached that status, saved 25% for themselves even if some of their bills didn't get paid on time! They paid themselves first, regardless.

3. TAKE ACCEPTABLE INVESTMENT RISKS. This means you shouldn't be in commodities, junk bonds, etc. The rich, on their way to becoming so, don't accept risks of that magnitude. Later on in their financial cycle, they may speculate, but only in their investment specialty. They are in the market when the signs indicate they should be. They are into precious metals. They use their money market accounts when it's time to let-the-market-dust-settle. They use every one of these creative measures to continually maximize the use of their cash asset. They take risks that are well researched. They avoid most traditional investments. They avoid financial institutions for their investments in all but rare exceptions (for example, when short term TCDs were paying 16 to 20+% a few years back.)

4. CONTROL YOUR EXPENSES. Affluent people not only know how to make it, they know where every penny is or where it went. In my conversations with wealthy people, this subject was referred to most often as the one area where the average person goes wrong.

The sad, boring truth is, you have to have a budget, and you have to stick to it. You have to maintain your own personal bookkeeping system. The bottomline? It's not only what you make, it's what you do with what you make. You cannot ignore your expenses and expect to be rich. Many people who should be rich, based on their income, aren't because of a failure to understand the relationship between wealth and expense control.

5. CONTROL YOUR INVESTMENTS. Rich people universally retain hands-on control of their capital.

They may have a broker, an investment counselor, etc., but they run the show. They spend time on their investments, and they allow no position to become stagnant. They use their cash, use it again, and reuse it after that. They know that, like merchandise on the grocer's shelf, your capital has to turn-over to return the maximum.

Most of all they know that they have more to lose than any advisor they may listen to — and they act accordingly.

An interesting reaction I ran into on numerous occasions: many said they had a broker, and/or a counselor, etc., but, "They didn't know #$&#". They were simply used for reference or input that was then used or discarded by the asset's owner. This response was quite common. The rich believe they know more than the so-called experts. Judging by the results of their investment efforts, they're right. And they didn't acquire that attitude after the fact, they had it even when they were just starting out.

6. OVERLOOK NOTHING. A perfect example of this technique was revealed on a review of what millionaires did prior to becoming millionaires, while they were still employed by others. Most employees don't know all there is to know about company investment benefits. Many companies match your savings, through a company savings plan, dollar for dollar. Yet, many employees don't take advantage of such a high return investment. Other firms allow you to borrow at low or no interest rates. Still others have tax-free investment plans or stock option opportunities. Sad to report, many employees never take advantage of these high-return, tax-free company benefits.

On the other hand, a number of very wealthy people used these company opportunities as a springboard for their ultimate wealth. Many wealthy people had very humble beginnings. That's something to remember. The point of this example is, no matter what your financial status, you must overlook nothing at every stage. Make the most of every opportunity!

7. UNDERSTAND THE "RULE OF 72". The Rule of 72 allows you to immediately determine how fast any investment will double in value. Of course, you need an interest or return rate for this to work, but many investments do in fact have a stated or a historical return. The rule works like this: take whatever rate the investment offers and divide it into the number 72. The answer tells you how long, in years, the investment will take to double your asset value. This isn't precisely accurate, but it works for comparisons of investment opportunities. For instance, if a Time Certificate of Deposit offers 8%, it will take nine years for your investment to double (72 divided by 8). If a real estate deal promises 12% it will double in six years.

Of course, this doesn't take into account risk and other considerations, but it does work and has many applications. It gives a measure to your investment choices, and that's important.

8. NEVER BORROW FOR DEPRECIATING ASSETS. You can borrow for investments. You can borrow for your business. You can borrow for necessities (and then you should only spend and/or borrow the minimum necessary). But never borrow for depreciating assets. To do so is counterproductive to amassing wealth.

The reality of this advice can be felt if you'll add such a purchase to your personal financial statement. For instance, if you buy a car and have to borrow $10,000.00 for forty-eight months at current interest rates, you have created a liability of approximately $13,500.00. On the asset side you have created an asset worth, after you drive it a week, approximately half what you paid. In effect, you lost the difference between the liability and the asset. In this case, approximately $7,000.00. That's what happens with each borrowing for depreciating assets. Negative net worth, not wealth.

9. KNOW HOW TO BORROW. Why? Because on your way up the ladder of wealth, you're going to owe more than you have saved. Which means, at least for a time, you will have more interest expense than interest income.

First, there is the loss of money associated with interest expense. For example, by not negotiating your interest rate, you may lose a fortune in your mortgage. For example, a 2 percentage point reduction on a $100,000.00 thirty year mortgage will save you approximately $57,000.00 in repayments. That's money you could have used for investment purposes. Additionally, that loss could have tripled in value over the course of the thirty year mortgage. You see, knowing how to borrow money is important.

Perhaps more importantly, almost without fail, the wealthy at some point had to borrow money to make money. They cultivated the market so they could receive financing they might otherwise have been denied. They used a loan to get their business started, etc. You have to understand how to borrow money. You have to spend time ensuring your access to lending whenever you need it and/or the right opportunity comes along.

Statistically, becoming rich is becoming easier — that's encouraging. If you'll learn how to save for investment purposes and control your expenses, you'll be surprised at how quickly you can amass a sizable net worth. It appears that most fail in this regard because they want it all today. It doesn't work that way. That's not conjecture. That's the experience of people who have made it and made it big.

MAKING THE MOST OF EVERY DOLLAR

Every dollar that passes through your hands must be used to increase your income. Doing less is wasteful and foolish.

The best way to increase your return is to use one or more of the many accounts that pay interest on a daily basis. Settle for nothing less than day-of-deposit-to-day-of-withdrawal, compounded and paid daily interest on all your accounts. This maximizes your net return. Many people opt for so-called sophisticated accounts that sound good but, because financial institutions are allowed varying methods of interest computations, return very little to your bottomline. Don't be fooled by advertising. Put a pencil to the net return before making an account choice. Of course, you must also compare service fees on accounts as some, while offering a fair interest rate, take back that and more in account fees. Clearly, comparison shopping is called for in today's complicated financial marketplace.

Here are some additional tips that will help you squeeze every cent out of every dollar:

1. NEVER ACCUMULATE IDLE CASH. Don't delay in depositing checks. The sooner you deposit them, the sooner they will be collected and you can start earning interest.

Don't save cash around the house. If you aren't going to use that money within a few days, it should be in an interest-bearing account.

When you go on vacation, don't forget to immediately deposit any unused traveler's checks.

Don't buy official checks prior to when they are actually needed. Many people buy a cashier's check for a major purchase days or weeks before the transaction is completed. That's the same as having idle cash in your pocket.

2. DON'T OVERWITHHOLD YOUR TAX OBLIGATION. Many people do this while referring to the principle

as their forced-savings account. Some overwithhold because
they don't want to be stuck with a gigantic tax deficit at the
end of the year. While still others know if they have it they'll
spend it.

While I understand the motivation(s) that might entice
one to overwithhold, it's a big, costly mistake. Take a few
minutes to accurately determine your future tax obligation
and adjust your withholding accordingly. The savings should
be put in an interest bearing account.

You're probably paying too much in taxes already. Why
pay more? The IRS doesn't pay interest on tax withholding
excesses. Additionally, you may have to wait months to receive your refund.

3. PAY YOUR BILLS AT THE LAST MINUTE. If you
pay your two hundred dollar winter electric bill three weeks
before its due date, you've lost three weeks worth of interest
on two hundred dollars. Multiply this principle of early bill
paying by every bill you have for the entire year. The use of
money on huge sums are lost due to this practice.

Your credit rating doesn't improve by paying early. In
this example, all you accomplish is giving your utility company interest that could have been yours.

There is a great deal of income to be made by paying
your non-interest accruing bills at the last minute. Therefore, never pay your bills on time. Pay them at the very, very
last minute.

4. WORK YOUR MONEY. Don't just stick that money in
a passbook account. While that's better than nothing, you
can do even better. Most families should consider a NOW or
SuperNOW Account, a Money Market Deposit Account, Time
Certificates of Deposit, US Savings Bonds, T-Bills, and all
other liquidity available accounts. Find those right for you
and combine them into a personal cash flow system that offers the best possible interest rate return.

If this sounds complicated, it's not. Actually, it's more
time consuming than complicated. But, once you've decided
on your account combination(s), even time isn't a problem

and it's just a matter of a few minutes a week to maximize the use of your cash.

Depending on your financial circumstances, you may be losing a substantial sum of money by misusing your cash. My estimate is that the average family loses one to three hundred dollars a year.

That may not sound like much, but over the years it adds up, especially if you invest the savings. Let's use the lower estimate, one hundred dollars, and see what it amounts to over a forty year financial lifetime. One hundred dollars is an average of $8.33 per month. If we invest that added income every month for forty years at an average interest rate of nine percent, what balance do you think you will have? The answer is a most impressive $38,995.40. Let's use the larger estimate of three hundred dollars. That's $25.00 a month. At the same average return and term, nine percent over forty years, you will have earned an almost unbelievable $117,033.01. This is a clear example of the principle I keep harping on: it's important to save money, but more important to use those savings for a greater return.

Even if your financial lifetime is substantially less than forty years, the added income will be worth the effort of maximizing your cash. It's a simple and profitable habit to get into.

FAMILY FINANCIAL CHECKLIST

To be productive, a family's finances must be run like a successful business. You have to make the same tough decisions and apply the same objective criteria to the family budget that you apply at the office. It's too bad most families don't realize this important fact.

Without moralizing, let's get to the specifics. The following checklist should be reviewed on a regular basis by all family members who have an input into the bottomline.

1. FINANCIAL STATEMENT. You should commit a financial statement to writing. How else are you going to know how you're doing financially?

By updating your financial statement, you can see your financial progress as your net worth increases. If things are going in the opposite direction, you'll be able to see that, too, and thereby be able to change direction.

2. BUDGET. Without a budget, your finances are doomed. A budget tells you where you've been, where you are, and where you're going. It's the most important aspect of family financial management.

The budget will include a review of your income, debts, expenses, etc. It should account for every penny, because, as affluent people know, it's not what you make that counts, but what you do with what you make that's important.

Most significantly, a budget, properly written and followed, will give you resources for your investments.

3. THE BACK-UP. Every family should have a back-up or contingency plan in case circumstances change dramatically.

For instance, if you lost your job this afternoon, how long would your family be able to survive while you were looking for other employment? If you became disabled for an extended period of time, would you be able to manage financially?

A back-up plan will help answer any and all such questions before the fact, which is the best way to survive a financial catastrophe. Pre-planning is never a waste of time.

4. INSURANCE. The major mistake most families make on this subject is ignoring it. They take out their insurance needs and forget it. They have life, accident, home owner's insurance and whatever, but they forget that things seldom remain the same.

With inflation your home value has increased. Has your coverage? Ask the same question with all your coverages. You don't want to be insurance poor, but you don't want to be underinsured either.

Perhaps most important these days is health insurance. Add up your coverage at work (if any) with your private coverage. Is it sufficient? With the escalating health care costs you must keep current. If, as an example, you have to pay the first $1,000 plus 20% of any medical, you may have an alarming bill if you have a major medical crisis. In many parts of the country hospital beds are $1,200 per day, and that's before any medical treatments or tests. The point is, you cannot afford any gaps in coverage.

5. RETIREMENT PLANS. Do you know what your entire pension plan(s) will add up to at your retirement? If not, you're headed for trouble.

What about Social Security? Forget it. The system is statistically bankrupt. If it's still there when you retire, it will be a bonus.

Do you have a Keogh plan? An IRA? Did the Tax Reform Act of 1986 affect your retirement plans? Will future tax changes affect your plans?

Planning for retirement is becoming more and more of a problem. Why? Because the government keeps changing the rules along the way. How can you plan when you don't know what the rules will be? You can't, and that in itself gives you direction. How? Plan on diversification for retirement. That way one or two changes in the law or taxes will only affect a portion of your plan. The basics will still be left in place.

The only thing you can plan on for sure is that the government will not help your retirement efforts.

6. FINANCIAL RELATIONSHIPS. Review your bank, savings and loan, brokerage house, investment planner, etc. These financial relationships change as your finances change. Yet most never move their accounts unless something major happens. That's a mistake.

Every financial relationship mentioned above works for you. And, as such, you have to treat them like an employee. In that light, should they be talked to? Should they be fired? Unfortunately, most families have things backwards. They feel the bank is in charge. Their investment advisor is too, and so on. Again, they work for you. Demand results. Check their records with YOUR MONEY! If you don't like the review, it's time to move on.

7. INVESTMENTS. When's the last time you reviewed all your investments? Your stocks, bonds, real estate, savings, collectibles, etc.?

Are they really all you hoped for? Are they stagnant? Are they no longer meeting your needs because your needs have changed?

Remember, all financially successful people have hands-on control of their investments. They review them constantly and make adjustments when necessary. While you don't want to overreact, you can't afford to ignore what is happening with the fruits of your labors.

8. WILLS. The average family member doesn't have a will. Those who do, make a will out once and never touch it afterward. Either scenario is unacceptable.

First, you need a will, because you're not going to live for ever. As crass as that sounds, it's true and needs to be said. Accidents happen, so even if you're young you need to make provisions for your family. If something happens to you, do you really want them to have the added burden of having to fight the lawyers and courts because you didn't meet your ultimate financial obligation? Of course not.

Those who have made provisions need to update. Perhaps you bought or started a business since your will was made out. That needs to be addressed in your will, as does any change of financial substance.

If you can't remember the last time you updated your will, it's probably time to update your will.

Reviewing your family finances is not optional. You cannot ignore your responsibility. To do so will ensure a substantial reduction in your bottomline.

I mention this because of what I see daily in my consulting work. The vast majority of financial problems are caused by ignoring one's finances. Most such difficulties could be avoided with a little time and effort. This checklist will help remind you of those areas on which you should concentrate.

The fact is, you wouldn't run your business finances haphazardly, and you shouldn't do so with your personal finances either. Strangely enough, many extremely successful business people can't or don't even balance their personal checkbooks. Imagine what other important family financial issues they're ignoring. That's a costly judgement mistake, because the real bottomline IS AT HOME.

RECORD KEEPING

Record keeping is one of the more annoying aspects of our financial and personal life. That's probably why most of us don't bother. Often times this careless attitude costs us money, or our family additional grief in a crisis.

Are you guilty of ignoring this important responsibility? One can only make that determination in a worst case scenario, so here goes: if you died, would your family be able to locate all your financial records, important papers, debtors, creditors, tax records, etc.? You should be able to answer in the absolute, not a qualified positive. If you can't, it's time for some preventive maintenance.

Obviously, one doesn't have to die to have the need for proper record keeping. Unfortunately though, in most instances, this necessity is not good news. Some examples: divorce, lawsuit, accident, illness, fire, or theft. At some time in your life you may suffer one of the above, which means you can't ignore the warning that record keeping is required. It should also be clear to heads of households that your family will need all the help they can get if you're incapacitated. You should plan to lessen their grief and anxiety.

There are four basic systems you need to have a complete workable file. Don't let that put you off. Each one is quite simple and takes very little time to set up, even less to maintain.

1. INVENTORY. A household inventory file with pictures of the more expensive items.

The reason is obvious. In case of fire, theft, or other insurance claims, it will make your contact with the insurance company substantially less adversarial.

Additionally, when completed and you assign a replacement value to each item, you may find out that you are over or underinsured, which may be a bonus for your effort, because being overinsured does nothing for you. Insurance companies don't pay claims on a policy basis per se, they pay on relative worth (unless you have a replacement policy).

Simply stated, if you insure furniture for $10,000.00 and it only has a replacement value of $7,500.00, all you are going to get paid is $7,500.00 in case of loss. You will have paid a premium, for the additional $2,500.00, for nothing. The same principle applies to other insured possessions.

The reverse is also true. You don't want to be underinsured, as, here too, you will ultimately experience a loss.

Specifically, your home inventory should include a room by room listing of assets. Be as complete as possible —include date purchased, purchase price, brand name, description of condition, etc. — and then include a picture.

Once completed, this listing will simply have to be updated, which will only take minutes a month.

2. HOME FILE. No business would think of existing without a filing system. No home should be without one either, because, in a real sense, your family finances are a business, or at least should be treated that way.

Invest in a medium size file cabinet, which will probably be more than adequate. Be sure it's lockable.

You want to keep separate files of:

a. INCOME TAX RECORDS.

b. BANK STATEMENTS — including canceled checks.

c. INSURANCE POLICIES — separated by company and purpose.

d. WARRANTIES — for expensive items such as appliances (purged as warranties expire).

e. SOCIAL SECURITY INFORMATION — for each family member.

f. LOAN DOCUMENTATION — mortgage, credit cards, etc.

g. HOME INVENTORY.

h. SAFE DEPOSIT BOX INVENTORY — I don't recommend using a safe deposit box, but if you do, maintain a listing.

i. WILLS — for each family member.

j. BILLS — paid and unpaid.

k. MISCELLANEOUS — use this category as your catch-all. Each family has its own requirements. Maybe you need employment files. Others may have an educational file for their children.

3. SAFE OR SAFE DEPOSIT BOX. You should avail yourself of a safe deposit box or an in-home safe. It should be used to safeguard irreplaceable items, those with a high value in real money or sentiment, and papers that prove ownership. House title, mortgage documents, stocks, bonds, passbooks, marriage license, contracts, are all examples of what may be included.

4. THE "WHERE" RECORD BOOK. This is a record of where your other records are kept, coupled with a short list of all important papers; i.e., insurance policy numbers, etc. It should be immediately available to your family in case you are incapacitated. So there are no misunderstandings, keep it simple. Locate it outside of your home, as it must be available if all other records are lost or destroyed.

Don't forget to give additional information on where those items not located in your file system can be located. For example, your will if it's located at your attorney's office.

Record keeping is no fun. It's one of those things you spend time on with no immediate benefit.

Yet, when needed, it can be replaced by nothing else. It will help you, it will help your family. Often times, at a crucial moment, it will mean the difference between profit and loss. In some cases, assuming a medical condition and therefore a medical file, it can mean life or death. I can't overstate my case.

I can guarantee that a good home filing system will more than pay for itself.

HOW TO PREPARE A BUDGET THAT CAN MAKE YOU RICH

Running a household is the same as managing a corporation. Monetary volume differs, but the principles behind success or failure are identical. If you are to become wealthy, you have to be as successful with your finances as General Motors is with theirs. This simple but critical fact is something the average person seldom understands.

There are two primary reasons why a company fails: (1) They are undercapitalized, or (2) they have poor management. While obviously intertwined, if you examine both, you'll realize that undercapitalization plays the major role. The point is: a poorly run business can oftentimes survive if it has enough capital, but a great management team, in spite of their expertise, will more than likely fail if there is insufficient capital.

Successful companies didn't start out that way — they began as an idea put in motion by aggressive managers. They took calculated chances. They invested, and then reinvested, time, effort, and money. They expanded when money, market, and conditions allowed. At times, they pulled back and waited. They seldom forced their market — they used the market. Planning, planning, and more planning. Without it, even abundant capital can be inadequate. It took years and consuming dedication. And that's what it takes for you to be successful. Unfortunately, the financial strategy of the average family would cause most companies to go broke within a year. In many instances that's because people are trying to become rich overnight. They want it now, forgetting that haste makes waste.

Do you have a financial plan? Do you update it every year?

If you expect to be wealthy, you must start making plans and taking actions that will lead to that eventually. With a realistic schedule and personal dedication almost everyone can become rich. We won't all be affluent to the same degree, but we can acquire resources far in excess of what might otherwise be expected.

To maximize wealth you have to be able to take advantage of investment opportunities. For that you need usable cash. And to have usable cash you must have complete control of your finances. Fiscal success is a two-pronged spear. First, you must exploit your income. Secondly, you must exploit the resources left after you pay your living expenses. If you're just making ends meet, you can't progress. In fact, with an inflation factor, you're not even retaining the status-quo.

Back to our corporate examples: every profitable company has a monthly, quarterly, and yearly budget. You should too. To that end, there are two documents you must prepare: a Profit & Loss (P&L) Statement and a Wealth Creating Budget. A P&L Statement is simply a reflection of where you are now; i.e., your income minus your expenses.

A P&L Statement is useless unless it leads to our budget; without the latter, the former can't offer solutions. A Wealth Creating Budget is the plan that will start you on the road to financial independence. It outlines how things will happen, it takes control.

The best way to explain this concept is by example. First, I have prepared a P&L Statement for a mythical family. Then, with a Wealth Creating Budget, I have, using the same income base, made adjustments that turn their losing situation into a winner.

MONTHLY PROFIT & LOSS STATEMENT
($50,000 INCOME, FAMILY OF FOUR)

YEARLY GROSS	$50,000	HOUSING	$800
MONTHLY GROSS	$4,167	REAL ESTATE TAXES	125
		FOOD	600
		TELEPHONE	150
		UTILITIES	250

		CAR	400
		INSURANCE	150
		MEDICAL (assumes employer hospitalization plan)	100
		ENTERTAINMENT	250
		OTHER (Itemize)	
		CREDIT CARDS	350
		PERSONAL LOAN	100
		MISC.	150
		SAVINGS	0
		FEDERAL, STATE & SALES TAX	1,042
TOTAL INCOME	$4,167	TOTAL EXPENSES	4,467
DEFICIT	300	SURPLUS	0
TOTAL	$4,467	TOTAL	$4,467

Even the casual observer can see this family has problems. They're barely able to keep things together and clearly they'll never be able to save money. Some things must be changed. The answer is percentage budgeting. (Before explaining, I have to recommend, since some budgetary items such as food, insurance, and housing, cannot be adjusted as easily as others, realign those that allow latitude and/or those that must be changed.) In our example, it's imperative this family start saving money. To arrive at that goal, I worked backwards; i.e., I determined the desired savings figure (based on the appropriate percentage), plugged it into the budget, and adjusted other items (based on the appropriate percentages) to accomplish our objective. Of course, in this illustration the one thing we must do immediately is remove the deficit. The next consideration is savings.

To reduce a money-drain, you either increase income or reduce expenses. All budgetary decisions are that simple — notwithstanding the model of the federal government. As we have more immediate control of expenses, that's where I'll concentrate. To do so, I offer recommended percentages of a gross salary.

Percentage Budgeting

Housing	25.0%
Real Estate Taxes	3.0%
Food	12.0%
Telephone	2.0%
Utilities	7.0%
Car expenses	5.0%
Insurance	3.5%
Medical	3.5%
Entertainment	2.0%
Other	1.0%
Miscellaneous	1.0%
Savings	10.0%
Federal, State & Sales Taxes	25.0%
TOTAL	100.0%

These are general recommendations. Obviously they cannot be followed to the letter. However, they should be looked at as benchmarks. Others might disagree with my percentages, but they are often trying to balance a budget, nothing more. I am trying to balance the budget and create wealth.

As with all financial advice, you have to pick and choose what is appropriate. For example, if you're locked-in to a mortgage that takes 40% of your income you'll have to radically adjust my other suggestions. That's OK, just as long as you remember the bottomline, which is to better use your income to produce more income.

Let's prepare a Wealth Creating Budget for our example family using our percentages.

WEALTH CREATING BUDGET (MONTHLY)
($50,000 INCOME, FAMILY OF FOUR)

YEARLY GROSS	$50,000	HOUSING	$1,042
MONTHLY GROSS	4,167	REAL ESTATE TAXES	125
		FOOD	500
		TELEPHONE	83
		UTILITIES	292
		CAR	208
		INSURANCE	146
		MEDICAL (assumes employer hospitalization plan)	146
		ENTERTAINMENT	83
		OTHER (Itemize)	42
		MISC.	42
		SAVINGS	416
		FEDERAL, STATE & SALES TAX	1,042
TOTAL INCOME	$4,167	TOTAL EXPENSES	$4,167
DEFICIT	0	SURPLUS	0
TOTAL	$4,167	TOTAL	$4,167

Notice, there are some startling differences between this and the P&L Statement — differences that offer some interesting conclusions. This family is well within our housing percentage, in fact they show a surplus, which makes getting their finances in order rather simple. They should try and reduce their food expense. Their car expense is too high —

they may wish to sell their present car and buy one more in line with their financial status. And they should try and pay off their credit card and personal loan debt as soon as possible. Other expenses are slightly out of line, indicating they must start using across-the-board discretional restraint. But, these are small adjustments that can be accomplished with ease. It's worth their effort because a Wealth Creating Budget offers entry to investment opportunities they would otherwise have to forego.

Unfortunately, there are instances where percentage budgeting will call for substantial life style changes. I hope, when you put a pencil to your budget, nothing that drastic is called for. If by chance it is, you must consider the consequences of taking no corrective action; i.e., you've doomed your family to financial failure. With that being the bottomline, there really isn't a choice. How you arrive at the right monetary mix is not important, but the principle(s) cannot be challenged.

There was a time when the-live-for-today, deficit spending types were rewarded. They would buy a home they couldn't afford and justify it because, due to runaway inflation, they were paying back the mortgage with "cheaper dollars." They used the same philosophy with every purchase they couldn't afford. With inflation in double digits, there was some perverted logic in their position. However, they gained little as they spent their new-found paper/inflation wealth on interest payments. But that's history — the days of letting an inflationary economy pay your future bills are, at least for now, over. Common sense is at a premium — it always has been, but not everyone was wise enough to realize it.

Sit down and prepare a Profit and Loss Statement. Use my percentages and prepare a Wealth Creating Budget. Compare the two and make the necessary changes. Stick to it. Your financial future depends on it.

CREDIT DANGER SIGNS

I am opposed to borrowing money for virtually all the usual reasons, because borrowed money is too often spent purchasing depreciating assets (assets that decrease in value with the passage of time). That is a detriment to your net worth. Obviously, however, there are times when borrowing is not only necessary, it is advisable. For instance, a home mortgage is judicious. For this discussion, let's assume you have legitimate reasons for purchasing the use of money. (Although that assumption is not statistically valid for, as my research shows, approximately seventy-five percent of nonessential consumer debt should not have been incurred.)

Over and above the reason for your debt, there is another consideration — are you overextended? There is a simple method of knowing if your obligations are in line with your ability to repay them. (Obviously, this ignores the issue of whether or not the borrowing was advisable.) This rule of thumb should be applied without rationalization. I say upfront, many will be shocked to learn they are overextended. Apply the formula and learn from the experience.

Take your after-tax income, subtract your housing and auto expense and multiply the remainder by 12%. The answer indicates the total additional outstanding debt you should have. Using this formula, most families appear to exceed their maximum. If yours is one of them, it's time for some changes, no matter how difficult.

Let's look at an example. A family with an after-tax income of $40,000.00 and housing and auto expenses of $1,000.00 per month should have a maximum additional debt of $3,360.00 ($40,000.00 - $12,000.00 x 12%). That figure should include all their installment debt, credit card balance(s), second mortgage, etc. Think the total is too small? Paraphrasing an old axiom, "Sometimes the financial truth hurts."

While this formula gives a clear picture of your present debt ratio, you should be aware of warning signs along the way. You've probably got credit problems if:

1. YOU ARE USING CREDIT TO PURCHASE EVERYDAY NEEDS. If you've started to use your credit card or cash advances to pay your rent, buy food, etc., you are in immediate serious financial trouble.

2. LOAN PAYMENTS ARE TAKING MORE AND MORE OF YOUR PAYCHECK. Under normal circumstances your debt-to-income ratio should be reducing or, at worst, being maintained. If yours keeps going up, regardless of salary increases, you must change your buying habits.

3. YOU CAN'T REDUCE YOUR LOAN BALANCES. If your credit card bill stays about the same every month, regardless of your payments, you are on a treadmill leading to financial distress.

4. YOU'VE STARTED TO PLAY GAMES WITH CREDIT. For example, you keep making purchases you can't afford by making smaller and smaller down payments and charging the rest. Or, you start paying one credit bill with a cash advance from another.

5. YOU RECEIVE PAST DUE NOTICES. A rather failsafe, undeniable method of knowing you're exceeding prudence.

Those who are overextended can't necessarily change their debt structure overnight, but that shouldn't stop them from making immediate efforts to correct matters. Remember, this recommended debt percentage is valid regardless of your income. How serious is the principle of understanding the relationship between controllable debt and the ability to generate personal wealth and financial security? It's critical. The point is made every time a former millionaire files bankruptcy. They had income, they had assets — what they didn't have was control of their debt.

Knowing you've got credit problems is the easy part. Doing something about it is the real measure. Too many choose the debt consolidation route. While that is an option, it's an expensive one; i.e., you're financing high-priced credit with high-priced credit. Your net interest expense can become astronomical. More importantly, too many use the debt consolidation route to get themselves in deeper. They acquire the loan with good intentions, but end up back at the easy credit trough within months. Clearly, the best way to quit abusing your finances is to cold turkey your use of easy, high priced credit.

For those who haven't reached critical mass on this subject, I remind them, as with all issues there are degrees. Using a credit card interest rate of 22%, if you're only $1,000.00 over your debt-to-income ratio, and assuming a financial lifetime of forty five years, it will cost you $9,900.00 in interest alone. That's the expense side of the ledger. Now let's look at the income side. If you had been saving/investing that $18.34 per month ($9,900.00 divided by 540 months) at 10% compounded over the same time span, you would have a balance of $192,144.26. As you can see, it's not only what you're paying in interest on excessive debt, it's what you're not earning with the money you're wasting that's important. And even a relatively small mistake can cost you a fortune.

HOW TO PROTECT YOURSELF FROM CREDIT CARD FRAUD

It is estimated that credit card fraud in 1988 totalled a half-billion dollars. Would it surprise you to know that the majority of that fraud was perpetrated against individuals who didn't lose or have their credit cards stolen? That's right. Most credit card fraud is accomplished simply by someone knowing your card number. Actually acquiring the card itself is not required. And that's why everyone, even the most careful, may end up being a credit card fraud victim — unless you protect yourself as follows:

1. CHECK AND DOUBLE CHECK YOUR BILL. Make sure all the charges are correct. If not, call the card company immediately. You're not liable for charges that don't belong to you, but you have an obligation to report misuse of your card. Failure to report fraud can cause difficulty in your credit relationship(s). In actual money, you are only obligated for $50.00 of fraud charges (a good reason to ignore credit card "insurance") — and in actual practice that is seldom enforced. (Debit cards are another matter entirely. In that case, if you don't report its theft or loss within two business days, you can be liable for $500.00. If you don't report the loss within two months you can be held liable for the full amount of your line with the bank. Obviously your PIN deserves additional cautions.)

2. NEVER SIGN A BLANK CHARGE RECEIPT. This can happen in many ways. For instance, if you're at a hotel where you'll be keeping a running tab you may be asked to sign in advance. You can see how dangerous that could be. While the practice is commonplace, you should politely refuse to do so. Settle your bill when it's due. Don't pay in advance with a signed blank receipt.

3. DESTROY CREDIT CARD CARBONS IMMEDIATELY. This is the principal method whereby credit card fraud artists acquire valid account numbers, expiration

dates, and signatures — all the specific information one would need to successfully use your card for their benefit.

While your monetary obligation is limited, you don't want to go through all the hassle of squaring things with the credit card company once fraudulent charges start appearing on your bill. Especially if it could have been avoided. Then, too, there is the extra time and effort spent getting a new card(s).

4. NEVER LOSE SIGHT OF YOUR CARD. Another area where cards are exploited is when they're illegally copied, or imprinted, by store clerks. If you're not watching your card at all times, the clerk may make a copy of the card and then sell it to the person who will actually commit the fraudulent charges. There is a big market in selling card imprints.

There is no reason for the clerk to go into the back room with your card. Don't lessen your vigil just because you're dealing with a store representative.

5. UNLESS YOU'RE PLANNING AN ORDER, NEVER GIVE YOUR ACCOUNT NUMBER OVER THE PHONE. A favorite and successful credit card scam is to call people at random (or from a bank or store customer list) and tell them that they have won a contest if their credit card number starts with, for instance, 4678. If yours does, the caller will ask for the rest of your number to "verify" your prize. They will also ask for the expiration date.

The trick is that all credit cards from a specific issuer, like your local area bank, have the same first four number prefix. The odds are pretty good that they will find a number of bank customers even by calling at random. With a listing, their odds improve dramatically. The fact that they "knew" your first four numbers gives them an added legitimacy many people fall for — not to mention the greed factor in winning a car or whatever.

It's best to remember that, unless you originated the call, don't give your card number out, no matter how tempting the offer.

You should never use a credit card to borrow money. They should only be used for convenience. That notwithstanding, they do offer some benefits that may induce your use (provided you pay your bill in its entirety). They offer protection in certain mail order purchases that isn't available if you pay by check, give an excellent means of expense accounting and, depending on your charge card's billing method, you may be able to use their money free of charge for a month or more.

As much as I dislike the way most people use their credit cards, I am aware that, if used correctly, they offer benefits that can be exploited to your benefit. But, if you are going to avail yourself of that possibility, you also make yourself available for credit card fraud. And it takes more than just keeping physical control of your cards. For added protection, I'd also suggest the following:

1. LIMIT YOURSELF TO NO MORE THAN THREE NATIONALLY RECOGNIZED CARDS. If chosen correctly, they will meet all your needs while limiting your work and monetary loss should you lose or have your wallet stolen. If you have three cards, the worst that can happen is you may owe $150.00. If you have ten cards you might owe $500.00.

2. MAKE COPIES OF YOUR CARDS. Copy them on one sheet of paper and record, under each card, the number to call in case the card is lost. Keep the reference listing at home in a safe place. This is the most convenient method of knowing where to call if your cards are lost, and what information to give when reporting to the card issuer.

3. HAVE ALL YOUR CHARGES END IN A SPECIFIC NUMBER. If you're charging something for $25.80, and you want all your charges to end in 5, charge $25.75 and give the clerk a nickel in cash. You can always add or subtract to ensure all your charges end in the same number.

The reason for this little trick is that it makes any fraudulent charge stand out like a large red flag, which will make your billing review that much easier.

Credit card fraud is something we all have to be concerned with. It costs us on a number of levels. First, we have to pay extra retail markup so stores can recover their credit card losses and then, if we're a victim, we have to be bothered correcting matters. As anyone who has lost their credit cards can tell you, it's an experience you can live without. It's frustrating, time consuming, worrisome, and sometimes costly. That's the bad news.

The good news is, with a little reasonable caution, you can ensure your credit cards are never used improperly.

CREDIT BUREAUS AND YOUR RIGHTS

Credit bureaus are a necessary fact of life. For example, without them acting as an informational clearing house, the long slow process of loan approval would be even longer and slower. They do serve a number of useful functions.

However, as anyone who has ever had difficulty can attest, an unprofessional bureau can wreak havoc with your finances. They can cause irreparable damage. They can cause your mortgage application to be denied, or your employment application to be refused, just to name two examples.

Most credit bureaus are professional and take their legal obligations seriously. However there are those that don't. Add to that the fact that even the good bureaus make mistakes, and you have a public at risk. In the case of credit, you have another serious problem, as transactions between banks and the bureau are normally kept secret. As such, the customer is seldom aware what possibly erroneous information the bureau reported that caused their application to be denied.

It is my belief, based on history and experience, that you should ASK TO SEE YOUR CREDIT FILE AT LEAST ONCE A YEAR! You need to verify the accuracy of the information the bureau will be forwarding to others. It is a lot easier to correct matters before the fact than trying after the damage has been done.

How can you contact your credit bureau? Look in the phone book under Credit Bureau or Credit Reporting Agencies. If you can't find the one with your file, call your bank and ask them what bureau they use. Chances are, since they are local, they will be using the one that has your file.

Call the bureau and tell them that you'd like to see your file. They will give you instructions on how their firm complies with the law. Many require a written request. Others will ask you to come in if you can. Some will send a form to fill out. Regardless of their approach, they must be "reasonable," so if they are not cooperating, you have recourse.

When dealing with a credit bureau, you'll probably find their response time to be excessive. So if you haven't received what you want within a few weeks, you should call or write again. Always keep copies of your correspondence as it may be needed later if there is a disagreement.

Let's review your rights:

1. YOU HAVE A RIGHT TO REVIEW YOUR FILE. This means you can actually see the file and a listing of all who have requested information in the file for the last six months.

The bureau has the right to charge a reasonable fee for this service, which normally ranges from $2.00 to $25.00.

They don't have to show you the file itself, but they do have to provide you with all the information contained therein. You and your spouse have a right to this information and the bureau has to provide a knowledgeable person to answer any questions you may have.

2. YOU HAVE A RIGHT TO HAVE INCORRECT INFORMATION REMOVED FROM YOUR FILE. Bureaus have to show reasonable care in verifying information in any file, but mistakes happen. If you see an error in your file bring it to their attention immediately. If they cannot justify the information as accurate, they must remove it.

If there is a dispute over a reported matter you can make a written explanation, giving your side of the circumstances. The bureau must then make your summary part of your credit report from that date forward.

If items are removed from your file, the bureau must make that information available to anyone who had requested a report on you within the last six months.

3. YOU HAVE A RIGHT TO HAVE NEGATIVE INFORMATION REMOVED FROM YOUR FILE. Bureaus are very lax in this regard. They quite often don't bother to meet the regulations that state bankruptcies must be removed af-

---

ter ten years. Arrests, convictions, tax liens, collection problems, etc., have to be removed within seven years. The time limits help protect prospective lenders, while at the same time giving the consumer a second chance.

But, bureaus forget to remove information, and while they will provide the date of a bankruptcy for example, the lender won't care if it happened fifteen years ago. All they'll remember is the BK, which means they will deny the application based on information that should have been expunged.

If you have had problems in the past, you'd better make a visit to the bureau about the time you feel the information should be removed. On their own, the bureau might not get the job done.

4. YOU HAVE IMMEDIATE RIGHTS IF YOU'RE DENIED CREDIT. When a lender sends a notice of denial of credit, they have to state a reason for their rejection. Most denials reference a credit bureau report.

If that happens, the lender has to give you the name and address of the bureau where the information was gathered. You have a right to review your file. You can actually see that file — and everyone who has requested information in the last six months. If you file a request to see your file within thirty days after being denied credit, you can review your file for free, no charge can be assessed. Additionally, the lender, if you request, must give you a specific reason for the denial. That will help you at the bureau; i.e., you'll know exactly what you're looking for and trying to correct an error becomes that much easier.

5. YOU HAVE A RIGHT TO HAVE ONLY LEGAL INFORMATION IN YOUR FILE. Credit bureaus sometimes get far astray with information in files. They'll jot down information they gathered from people who they talk to, or perhaps someone repeats a rumor about you to one of their employees. Many strange things have shown up on credit reports, so don't think it can't happen.

Legally, the bureau can only keep records that are a matter of public record, such as civil suits, legal judgements, bankruptcies, most legal proceedings, identification specifics, employment facts, credit history, etc.

If the credit bureau doesn't meet its obligations for correct reporting procedures, you can sue them for damages and costs. If you were denied credit or a job because of their error, you have a cause for legal action. This includes punitive damages, so we are talking about substantial litigation under certain circumstances.

If you believe you have a problem with a credit bureau, you will want a copy of the Fair Credit Reporting Act of 1971. A free copy may be obtained from the Federal Trade Commission, Consumer Protection Bureau, Pennsylvania Ave., & Sixth St. NW, Washington, DC 20580-0000. Phone: 202-326-3238.

Credit bureaus are a necessity in today's financial environment. Businesses need information, and they need it fast. Credit bureaus service that need.

They also make mistakes. Sometimes they are unprofessional. Regardless of the cause, many, many consumers are harmed by erroneous information each and every day. Most, because they don't know their rights and how the system works, never understand what happened or why. They never realize that they didn't get their mortgage because a bankruptcy by another person with the same name was recorded on their file. Or that they can cost you a job because a mistaken court record is in their records stating you were convicted of passing bad checks.

Many of you are probably thinking this could never happen or, if it did, it must be easy to correct. Wrong! Ask anyone who has had this type of problem and they'll tell you what a nightmare they experienced.

The only way to avoid this happening to you is to do preventive maintenance on your credit file. To do that, YOU

HAVE TO REVIEW IT PERIODICALLY AND ENSURE
ITS ACCURACY.

If you do find a problem, you have to act decisively to
get the bureau to correct the error. You have rights — know
and use them.

WILLS

Everyone needs a will. Yet, statistics show that only three out of ten have completed this important legal document before they die. The other seven individuals have left, in addition to the loss to their loved ones, a financial mess for their family.

Obviously, there are degrees of need in the area of wills; i.e., most college students have little property to be concerned with, while middle-aged parents of three have numerous legal considerations that need to be addressed. However, they both need wills.

For those who have reduced needs, there are will kits one can purchase. They are of the fill-in-the-blanks variety, and only take a few minutes to complete. They are thoroughly legal, cost as little as $10.00, and can be purchased at most stationery stores. Those with serious considerations need a lawyer. For the average family, the costs should not exceed $250.00. If you use one of the franchise legal firms, like Hyatt or Wards, the cost should be about $75.00. More complicated estates may cost as much as $1,500.00 and should be taken to a law firm that specializes in estate planning. In truth, while I recommend the services of a professional of some varying degree, you can personally write out a will on a blank piece of paper. While I don't advise that, it's better than nothing.

Regardless of what manner of will you prepare or have prepared, there are some basic considerations you may want to review in-depth:

1. BE CAREFUL WHEN SELECTING AN EXECUTOR OF YOUR ESTATE. It is my considered estimate that fully 90% of those selected (from the non-professional ranks) are completely unqualified. Unfortunately, most people choose their closest friend or relative, with little thought to their abilities. This is a serious mistake.

While the individual chosen in this manner may have the best intentions, your wishes will, more than likely, not be carried out.

The other side of this problem is the professional that is dishonest. Estates are robbed daily in this country. Disreputable lawyers charge so many fees and the like for administrating the estate that, by the time distributions are actually made to the heirs, there is little left. The court system is very lax in prosecuting these grave-robbers masquerading as attorneys, so exercise caution if you opt for a lawyer/executor.

2. IF YOU HAVE MINOR CHILDREN, CHOOSE A GUARDIAN FOR THEM. If you don't, the court will.

Do you really want our judicial system, with all its many flaws, deciding the immediate fate of your children? You cannot let this happen, so make your wishes crystal clear. Your will cannot be open to interpretation on this matter.

Make sure, once you decide on a guardian, that they are notified of your intentions. You should know in advance that they will accept the responsibility.

3. IF NECESSARY, YOU MAY HAVE NEED OF A TRUST ACCOUNT FOR YOUR SPOUSE, OR FOR YOUR CHILDREN IF, BY CHANCE, BOTH MARRIED PARTNERS ARE KILLED AT THE SAME TIME. Trusts can be initiated by a will, which then guides the heir's finances if they are unable or unwilling to do so on their own.

This is one of those areas that costs a great deal during will preparation, but it is well worth the expense considering the long-term good that can come from such foresight.

A trust can also help stop an executor from wasting assets or robbing your estate. Obviously, one must have a substantial estate for this to have merit.

4. BE COMPLETELY THOROUGH. For everyone's protection, account for every asset you have and want distributed.

Be general when called for — for example, if you are young, and not in any statistical or known danger of dying, it would be foolish to say that you will your 1986 Chevrolet to heir "X". Chances are that, by the time you pass away, you will have bought and sold many cars, and specific wording means that, unless you constantly change your will every time you change vehicles, your wishes and intentions will be lost to a technicality. Better that you will "the family car" to heir "X".

Conversely, be specific when called for — for example, if you have an asset that you know will be in the family for as long as you live, spell it out by name when willing it. That way there will be no confusion or hard feelings.

5. KEEP YOUR WILL IN A SAFE PLACE WHERE EVERYONE YOU WANT TO KNOW IS INFORMED OF ITS LOCATION. It does no good to have a will that cannot be found.

6. UPDATE YOUR WILL AS NECESSARY. Unless your life and finances have become unbelievably stagnant, you have no choice but to periodically review your will and account for your changing financial status.

A will made when you were just married at twenty three will not be adequate when you're forty five, have three children, and a net worth of a few hundred thousand dollars. Yet, that inappropriateness happens quite often, which, in effect, makes your will worthless.

While not germane to the will itself, I strongly recommend that you have an additional booklet for your family outlining what they should know in case of your death. The data should include all important family papers and documentation (marriage certificates, birth certificates, Social Security cards, car titles, mortgage documents, location of bank accounts, insurance contracts, stocks and bonds, etc.). The will is just one aspect of an overall plan for your family. This booklet will fill in the gaps.

It is to their benefit, both emotionally and financially, if
you have anticipated and planned for all contingencies.
Nothing is sadder than watching someone lose a loved one
and then realize, in addition to the emotional grief, they
have to experience a financial and legal nightmare because
the deceased made no effort to plan for the inevitable.

THE NO-COST WAY TO CHANGE YOUR WILL. It is
important to periodically review your will. The reason being,
things constantly change, and, too, over a period of time, it is
typical for one to forget exactly what's in his or her will. If,
when examining your will, you decide a change or changes
need to be made you will probably call your lawyer. That's
certainly a viable option, but, from a cost standpoint, perhaps not the best one. A lawyer's time is expensive, especially those who charge to the nearest half or full hour. Your
change may only take minutes, but your cost may be many
times that. Additionally, if you have a will, as we all should,
and are young, chances are it will have to be changed dozens
of times before actually needed. Can you afford the expense
of your lawyer's time every year or so for the next forty years
for a problem you can solve yourself? Even if you can afford
it, is it a wise expenditure?

Naturally, I am not suggesting ignoring your attorney if
you feel the need, and/or if your will is complicated. Do what
you feel best. That notwithstanding, it's important that you
are aware of the no-cost way to alter your will — a codicil. A
codicil is an addition or supplement to an existing will, that
subtracts from, adds to, qualifies, modifies, or revokes a
prior provision.

Codicils are used for minor changes. If you need a new
will, destroy your old one and start over, with or without
your attorney. A codicil, or a large number of codicils in this
instance, would not be prudent and will simply muddy the
waters when it comes to carrying out your financial intentions. To change your will with a codicil, consider these simple suggestions:

1. DON'T ALTER YOUR WILL. Leave the original text alone. Crossing out or writing in new sections or inserts will not accomplish the desired results. In fact, doing so may make the original will invalid.

2. ADD THE CODICIL TO THE END OF THE WILL. The codicil should be typed, without errors or corrections, below the last signature on the last page of the original will. If there isn't room, start a new page and staple the page to the will itself. You'll need a codicil copy for each existing copy of the will.

3. REFER TO THE WILL'S DATE. For example: "I hereby revoke paragraph seven (7) of my will dated December 3, 1978, and substitute in its place: (your own wording)." Another alternative: "I hereby cancel the bequest of my furniture to my daughter, Sally Smith, executed in my will dated December 3, 1978, and bequest it, instead, to my daughter Jackie Smith."

4. RECONFIRM THE ORIGINAL WILL. After you make the codicil change, make a declaration stating that you confirm all other parts of the original will. For example: "Having made this codicil, I reconfirm all intents of my will, dated December 3, 1978, not affected by this change."

5. HAVE THE SAME NUMBER OF WITNESSES. The codicil requires the same number of witnesses as the original will. They don't have to be the same people, just the same number. All witnesses have to sign the will/codicil in your presence and theirs, so don't let anyone leave before everyone is finished. To make it easy to locate your witnesses, have each write their address. They should also initial the codicil. It is also wise to have the codicil notarized, although not required in every instance.

While the above is not a guide, it does give an indication that you can, if you so choose, formulate a codicil by yourself without expensive legal assistance. However, I mention again, avail yourself of a professional if necessary. Of course,

if you do have an attorney who is concerned with your wel-
fare and fair billing, a codicil should cost very little for
preparation or review. My intent is not to tell you how to
prepare a codicil, but rather to make you aware of your options. A will and/or codicils do not have to be prepared by an
attorney to be legal — that's the point.

A good reference book, should you decide to go it alone,
is the *Simple Will Book*, by Dennis Clifford, Nolo Press.
There are others available in most libraries. Ask the librar-
ian. There are even computer programs available that will
write your will after you fill in a few blanks. Ask at your
computer store.

A codicil is as important as the will it modifies, so give
careful consideration to your objective and then the technical
procedure of preparation. If you decide to make a change,
you can do so at no cost.

INVEST IN FOOD?

Investing in food sounds like a ludicrous idea. No one, other than farmers and grocers, invests in food. Well, before you chalk this off as nonsense, consider: an investment in food can return 20% or more. How does that compare with your stock market return, local bank investments, etc.? Chances are, under normal circumstances, a food investment will return, two, three, or four times what traditional investments offer, and with virtually no risk. Maybe this is worth considering.

By investing in food, I mean the purchase of foodstuffs and household items prior to their actual need. Ideally, you should buy $X amount of additional food each week or month to be put in your food investment storehouse. Obviously, only those things not perishable are considered. For example, canned goods, breakfast food, household cleaners, toilet paper, grains, etc. You should, with little damage to the monthly budget, be able to acquire an added year's worth of food within two years. After that you will have a continuous rollover position; i.e., you will always be a year ahead. Storage is not a problem, especially if you have a basement. Most foods and household items are just as easily stored at your house as they are in a supplier's warehouse.

And what does this effort get you? In each of the last eight years, food and household items have risen in price from 12 to 30%. On average, for the typical shopper, yearly food costs have escalated 20% during that same time period. Unfortunately, many, when discussing inflation, use the rate as determined by the government. Unfortunately, that rate is understated for the normal family and their needs by as much as two thirds. Every grocery shopper in America knows that's true.

Let's put some numbers to this so you can see the return potential of a food investment program. If you spend $100 a week on food and household needs, you have a yearly total of $5,200.00. If you put that amount in the stock market you

might make the average of the market itself, which is minimal when compared to risk, or lose a bundle. Or, for example, if you open a bank account with that $5,200, at present
rates you'll earn as little as $286.00 or as much as $429.00
depending on vehicle choice. But if you invest in food, you'll
earn at least up to $1,560 — free and clear — every year.
That's a remarkable difference. If investing in food didn't
sound so funny, you and every other investor would jump at
the opportunity. For example, instead of food, if we were
talking about a new stock or bond that would return 20% or
more a year with essentially no element of risk, you'd all be
pulling out your checkbooks.

By buying food and household items before the fact, you,
in effect, buy them cheaper, since by the time you do need
them they will have risen in price. This is a statistical, dependable trend that can't be ignored. Grocery store prices go
up each and every week. Seldom, except with seasonal
items, do they retreat (and that's not germane to this issue,
as seasonal items are perishable and wouldn't be considered
for a storage program).

To start a plan, I recommend the following:

1. Since most of us can't consider buying a full
year's supply at one time due to inconvenience and
cost, consider a 25 to 50% increase in your shopping budget, with the addition going to food investments. This will lessen the financial impact
and make the mechanics of acquiring a year's supply of items much easier. Remember, anything that
you typically use and can be stored is fair game.
Even some meats are canned, as is tuna fish, etc.
Overlook nothing, keeping in mind almost all
canned food stuffs have a shelf-life of up to two
years. If you're not sure of an item, ask the grocer
or write the manufacturer. In many instances,
household items escalate the fastest, so don't overlook their returns. Drain cleaner bought a year ago

works just as well as the stuff you purchased yesterday.

2. Rotate your stock. When appropriate, start using shelf stock and replacing it with today's purchases. That gives a fresh supply at all times and you'll never have to worry about shelf-life. Additionally, mark all food stuffs, indicating purchase date, to eliminate potential confusion.

My guess is that many readers are thinking this sounds like too much trouble to be bothered with. Well, it is slightly bothersome until you get the hang of it, and you may have to set up some storage shelves. Other than that, once you get started, it's quite simple. It's just like shopping for a larger family. You'll get used to it.

And for the effort, you receive the following benefits:

1. For the average family, you can expect a yearly dollar return of $1,000.00 to $1,500.00 on your investment once you complete your inventory and start using the stock. Apply that to ten, twenty, thirty years and you can see this is an idea that shouldn't be dismissed. Of course, as you will be replenishing your supply, you are a victim of rising costs at the checkout counter. However, you save money at the consumption stage, and that is where your return on investment is measured.

2. You have insured your family against numerous negative events. For example, if you lose your job you'll have a year's supply of food and household items to help ease the financial crunch. And you have also insured your family against a catastrophe such as a collapse of our food delivery system or government. Of course, those are spectrum extremes, but they could happen.

One thing I must mention to be complete, and that's the need to find as many wholesale shopping outlets as possible within your market area. The majority of your food and household stock should be bought in this manner, which will dramatically escalate my estimate of total savings. You should be able to add another 10 to 15% to your net if you take some additional time in shopping. You'll be combining present day savings with the return to be realized a year from now — the total could exceed 40%.

Investing in food and household items, on its face, may sound like a ridiculous idea. I hope we have convinced you it's not. With retail costs going up every day, it makes sense to try and find ways to lessen the impact on your budget's bottomline. This concept, pre-buying, is applicable to many circumstances and with many different items. If you know you will use a consumption item in the future, doesn't it make sense to buy it now at a lower price than it most assuredly will be sold for next year?

Unfortunately, too many ignore day-to-day finances and devote their efforts to more sophisticated considerations, like the stock market. That's a mistake in priorities, as most families real bottomline is their everyday existence. That's why I am introducing the concept of investing in food. Once instituted, you'll always be a year ahead of the inflation curve with a large portion of your budget, in addition to having a year's insurance policy on food and household goods. Put in that light, investing in food doesn't sound like such a crazy idea.

SURVIVING A FINANCIAL COLLAPSE

Most Americans don't believe a financial collapse is possible. That's understandable in light of the fact that, for all but the oldest, prosperity is all we've known. Granted, there have been recessions, but, compared to the rest of the world, things have been stable, and for the most part, profitable. Our standard of living has consistently improved, and things like the Depression are left to history books. Surely, that can't happen again. That's why we have the Fed, the FDIC, a managed economy, and so on. But, are you absolutely sure a worst-case scenario is no longer economically possible? I, while not a gloom-and-doom sayer, regretfully inform you that a collapse, while not imminent, is possible. What is more likely is a form of severe recession and a number of years of austerity and hard times.

Regardless of what you believe, and that includes those who feel good times will last indefinitely, you should have some contingency plan. Things don't have to reach the crisis stage for one to take advantage of monetary preplanning. That principle is why we buy insurance. For instance, we recognize the possibility that a very costly medical emergency could occur and we take actions to lessen its impact on our finances. That only makes sense. Yet, on a much larger scale, that of a total or partial collapse of our economy, we make no plans whatsoever. Do you really trust those in charge that much? Are you that enamored of Washington? Remember now, these are the same people who have given us a national debt of over THREE TRILLION DOLLARS! Being completely rational still leaves one with the distinct and unpalatable fact that, based on their track record, those in control of the economy don't know what they are doing, so it is not a stretch to anticipate possible problems down the line. That's all I'm saying. Again, I don't feel it's time to panic, like so many in the field have done in the past and are doing now. But, I am uncomfortable enough to warn that precautions are in order. It is only prudent to act on all the obvious signs.

I recommend a survival resource of one to three months worth of expenses, and to have that in the form of gold and/or silver bullion or bullion coins. The reason for hoarding hard currency is obvious in that, if a partial or full collapse does occur, paper money will become in reality what it is in principle, worthless.

Where should you save this reserve? In your home. Why there instead of the bank? Again, the answer is obvious. In a collapse, and at this point you should remember the condition of the banking and savings and loan industry, your safe deposit box may be sealed by governmental order, which means your gold and silver would be inaccessible. Your deposits, if they were worth anything, may suffer the same fate as in 1929, and/or you may have to wait months or years to be able to withdraw the funds. Check your savings and checking agreements with the bank. They state clearly that this is a possibility, so you shouldn't be surprised that I mention it. And finally, on this point, the FSLIC is bankrupt and the FDIC has but 27¢ for every $100.00 they "insure". Are you comfortable with that reserve percentage? That is the equivalent of you asking a bank to loan you $3,703,703 on a $10,000. home. What would their answer be? Exactly! They know those percentages offer no security, especially in these days when the banking system is close to being catastrophic.

I feel compelled to once again state my perspective. A COLLAPSE IS NOT AN UNDENIABLE FACT, BUT RATHER A DISTINCT POSSIBILITY. Regardless, to what level do things have to degenerate for your survival cash to be of use? In truth, not much. If nothing more than double digit inflation returns, these reserves will substantially appreciate in value. If we have a recession and you're without work, your reserve's merit will become readily apparent. If we do have a depression, these reserves will be a lifesaver. The bottomline is, no matter what the circumstances, no matter how severe, a hard currency reserve will be of value. It's a no-lose, win/win situation.

As I said, your reserve should be in a form of gold or silver. You'll find that silver dimes, quarters, and half dollars are an excellent medium. Gold coins will also suffice as they are now able to be purchased in small denominations (affordable to all). Both are easy to buy. Both are easy to hide.

Once you make your determination regarding what and how much to reserve, you are then faced with the task of successfully hiding same. This isn't as hard as it sounds.

You can buy any number of home safes that are fire proof and will withstand most burglary attempts. These safes are relatively inexpensive and you shouldn't have to spend more than two to three hundred dollars.

Of course, you don't have to go to the expense and trouble of installation at all if you don't want to. There are a million safe places around your home that will offer just as much security. Walls, baseboards, attics, pots for plants, and so on. If you use such tactics, make sure everyone in your family who should know your reserve location(s) does. If you're not available in an emergency, your security intentions will be lost, as well as the actual reserve. DON'T FORGET this most important aspect!

Should you be wondering about inviting a robbery by having such a reserve stored at home, if you don't tell anyone about your reserve, your odds of being robbed can't possibly be expanded. You'll stand the same chance as others in your neighborhood. And even if the worst happens, if you've hidden your reserve well, it's safe. Burglars don't have the time or inclination to look in attics and rip out walls.

Fire presents another problem. However, if you have opted for a safe, and assuming its fire rating is adequate, this no longer becomes a concern. If you decide simply to hide your reserve around the house, you can buy fire-safe mini-safes that can hold your coins. These small boxes can be held in your hand and work perfectly. Here again, you can all but eliminate the fire hazard.

A hard currency reserve valued at what you can afford is not a crackpot idea. IT IS A NECESSITY BASED ON CURRENT ECONOMIC CONDITIONS.

More than likely your reserve will never be used, and in that case it will just be a good investment. Look at this subject like any insurance matter. Apply the same standards you would with life insurance, health insurance, car insurance, liability insurance, your retirement IRA, and so on, and then try and explain how you can afford to ignore the largest need for insurance, that being an economic collapse. If we do have a collapse, all your other insurance will be worthless. A survival reserve is the one insurance that will be available when all others have failed.

The importance of this matter cannot be overstated. Ask anyone who went through the Depression how their life would have been different had they had thousands of dollars of hard currency at their disposal. At worst, they would have fared well — at best, they would have become rich.

Does history repeat itself? On the chance that it does, it makes sense to be prepared.

RIPPING OFF THE ELDERLY

One of the main targets of violent crime is the elderly. That unfortunate fact cannot be denied. Crime statistics continue to make the point.

Why? Because violent criminals know that in most cases the elderly will not, or cannot fight back. They are easily assaulted. And too, even if the criminal is caught, the elderly often are so ill or afraid they will not pursue the matter through the courts. There are many criminals who specialize in crimes against the elderly for that very reason, which is one more indication that our society is in decline. Clearly the elderly are at an ever-expanding risk.

It is not too surprising then that white collar criminals and con-artists would at some point also recognize the potential of ripping-off the elderly. And that's exactly what's happening. The elderly have been targeted by another group that has every intention of doing them harm. In this case the damage will be more financial than physical, but it should be mentioned that often after an elderly person has lost all their money to a scam, they end up having severe physical problems caused by the experience.

At any rate, I am interested in helping the elderly avoid financial scams. If you're not elderly yet, and therefore think you don't have to worry about this problem, think again. Unless you know something the rest of us don't, you'll eventually have this problem — it's just a matter of when. Additionally, while this information may not pertain to you now, it may help you help your parents. While I wouldn't presume to tell anyone what their relationship to their parent's financial circumstances should be, I can state that many scams against the elderly could have been avoided if the children had taken a few minutes to offer their parents prudent financial advice or been willingly available for reference.

Let's look at a few commonly used scams targeted at the elderly:

1. INSURANCE. Of course the elderly need all the insurance they can reasonably afford, but is it wise to buy from a commercial you heard on television, from an ad in the mail, a cold telephone call, someone selling door-to-door? The answer is a resounding NO!

If you want to discuss your insurance options you should initiate contact with varying reputable agents or agencies, so you can compare costs and benefits.

Of course, the best time to make insurance decisions is long before you retire, but things don't always work out ideally. Regardless, most insurance plans being sold by celebrities and the like are overpriced and perhaps worthless. They sound inexpensive, but the prices they quote are for a unit, which may be as little as $1,000.00 of coverage. If you want more you have to multiply the unit cost times the amount needed. For example, if coverage is only $5.98, but is for an undisclosed five thousand dollar unit, you would have to multiply that times ten to get the monthly cost for $50,000.00 coverage. That would be $59.80 per month or $717.60 per year for very little coverage. Then too, many of these policies have a large number of exclusions and conditions.

These life "insurances" are sold with a come-on, and then the cost is run up in the hopes the buyer will never understand exactly what has been bought.

This same technique is used for varying disability coverages. So caution is once again required.

Regardless of what type insurance you're buying, after comparison shopping, buy from a reputable agency ONLY!

2. GET RICH QUICK. There are so many of these operators around that it's hard to keep track of what scams are presently popular. There's buying precious metals, commodities, rare coins, real estate property, off-shore banks, oil drillings, etc.

That's not to say that any or all of the above are not legitimate in and of themselves. It's the disreputable and illegal use of the investments that has turned investment fraud into a multibillion dollar business. That's the problem.

More specifically, these get rich quick operators have focused on the elderly. They spend a great deal of time and money acquiring lists of names, addresses, and phone numbers of affluent older individuals and couples.

Don't think these operators aren't good at what they do, because they are. They could, as the old saying goes, sell ice boxes to the Eskimos. They are so good that many victims have to admit, after the fact, that they knew they were being taken, but just couldn't stop being part of the events the operator was controlling.

It is impossible to dissect all the financial scams being perpetrated today, so I won't try. The fact is, no matter what the investment, the scenario is always about the same.

Don't invest with anyone or any firm unknown to you personally. And don't invest with those who contact you through the mails or on the phone.

3. HOUSING/CARE. Many elderly have concerns about how they will be taken care of in case they can no longer afford their home and/or they become disabled. That leads us to home equity credit lines or reverse mortgages, and life-care contracts.

Since many elderly people have their homes paid for, there are those in the financial industry who offer "income" to the home owner, provided a home is pledged as collateral. In some cases the loan is a straight, or second mortgage. In others, it's a reverse mortgage whereby the lender starts making monthly payments to the borrower as a supplement to their available Social Security and/or retirement income.

The problem with these loans is that they are often grossly overpriced, having many, many associated fees, and in some cases are being offered by a middle-man who, while working with a reputable firm or bank, adds on additional finder's fees.

This area is not being abused as a fraud per se, but the result can be just as damaging. Only in rare cases would it be prudent for the elderly to borrow against their home equity. It sounds good, but it's not. A lifetime of work can be lost to a legitimate loan and its complexity that is designed to seize as much of your money as possible.

As a general rule of thumb, it is best for the elderly not to borrow on their residence. There are other safer, more profitable alternatives. Don't let a lender rape your finances, and subsequently your estate, by providing a loan that is not in your best interest.

Another housing consideration being offered around the country is life-care contracts. Basically, they are an exchange of money, property, etc., for the promise of care for the remainder of your life.

Here again, it's not the concept that's the problem, it's those who have found how easy it is to have the elderly give them all their money for a promise that the operator has no intention of keeping. Believe it or not, there are life contracts being offered and bought that provide care at institutions that aren't even built yet. The con-artists have brochures and the like, and they offer a chance to get in on the ground floor when prices are cheap. Unfortunately, they are all too successful. They can even sell something that they admit upfront is non-existent.

Life-care contracts may be an ideal solution to your concern regarding future care. However, visit the center, talk to those being served now, check with the state and federal governments regarding complaints and/or legal violations. Check on their financial stability. Remember, if they go bankrupt your life-care contract could become worthless.

Of course, never buy from a salesman who comes to you, as the beginning contract should be initiated by your needs.

Again, I can't cover all the illegal or immoral schemes being used against the elderly. There are just too many.

However, I hope the above examples help you understand a few of the more prevalent ones.

The following will help you protect your finances:

1. RECOGNIZE THAT IF YOU'RE ELDERLY YOU ARE A SPECIAL TARGET FOR INVESTMENT AND FINANCIAL SCAMS. And as such, you are perhaps five times more likely to be approached by a con-artist.

If you have living parents, understand their vulnerability and try to help whenever possible.

2. DON'T BUY OR INVEST FROM ANYONE WHO CONTACTS YOU COLD. Don't buy from a firm that advertises investments, insurance, etc., like they were advertising toothpaste.

3. DON'T BUY FROM ANYONE WHO MAKES PROMISES THAT ARE UNREALISTIC. That sounds so simple, but the results of investment scams say greed usually wins over common sense. Don't let that happen to you. For instance, it is impossible to speculate and receive a guarantee of safety and return. You know that. Don't let anyone tell you otherwise.

4. BEWARE WHEN YOU FEEL PRESSURED. Most swindlers want you to make a decision immediately. That's a red flag that shouldn't be ignored.

5. IGNORE REFERENCES THAT AREN'T KNOWN TO YOU PERSONALLY. Good cons have references that can be checked. Of course they are part of the scam. The point is, references are only as good as your ability to verify their legitimacy, which in most cases is impossible.

6. BE ALERT FOR UNPROFESSIONAL HINTS. For example, the salesman can't meet with you, you can't go to his office, correspondence is handwritten, a P.O. Box is his address, an answering machine answers when you call him, etc.

There are red flags with many scams. However, to be complete, it should be recognized that some are very high class. You cannot let your guard down just because of appearances.

7. CONTACT: *The American Association Of Retired Persons* (1909 K St. NW, Washington, DC 20049). Ask for their newsletter, *Senior Consumer Alert.* It outlines many of the more current scams and how they are being worked.

8. TALK TO YOUR FAMILY, FRIENDS OR OTHER TRUSTED FINANCIAL ADVISORS BEFORE MAKING A MAJOR MONETARY DECISION. Very often others can see the flaws, or point out areas of concern that you may have overlooked.

9. LASTLY, ACCEPT THE RESPONSIBILITY OF UNDERSTANDING THAT NO FINANCIAL FRAUD CAN BE SUCCESSFUL WITHOUT YOUR HELP. Unlike violent crime, you cannot be a casualty unless you willingly participate in assisting the perpetrator. The good news in that realization is that you have the ability to insure you are never a financial scam victim.

YOUR MAIL ORDER RIGHTS

Mail order shopping is a 60 billion dollar a year business that sells everything from vitamins to jewelry.

In the early days, catalog sales were aimed primarily at the rural community because of their geographic isolation. But that's changed. Now, every American family receives more than 60 catalogs per year. Of course, once you place an order with one mail order firm, your name gets sold to other mail order companies. It's the ultimate ripple effect or chain letter. That's why you receive so many catalogs you don't want and never requested.

With the expansion of mail order has come problems from firms that are either dishonest or unprofessional. In either case, they can cost you time, money, and untold aggravation. You do have some rights:

1. If the catalog doesn't give a time limit on when your purchase will be received, they only have 30 days from the date they received your order to make delivery.

2. If they do state a time limit, such as six to eight weeks, they must deliver your order by then.

3. They haven't met the time limit, whatever it is, until the order is complete and all components are received. Partial shipments do not qualify as meeting their obligation.

4. If the company cannot meet the time limit, they must notify the customer of their option of either receiving their money back or waiting until another stated time limit is reached. They will provide you with a return mail card to make your choice.

5. If they still cannot meet their new scheduled shipping date, they must return your money unless you are willing to agree to another delay as stated by a new delivery date.

6. At any time that you take a refund option, the company must return your money within seven business days of receiving your request. If you ordered by credit card, they must give you a return credit within one billing period.

These rules apply to products ordered through mail order, not over the phone, so don't confuse your rights if you have been solicited on the telephone. Additionally, there are some exceptions to your shipping rights. For instance, seed companies that ship by season are exempt. Magazines are another exemption example. You can see the reasoning behind their exemptions.

It should be said that most mail order companies are reputable firms that try to meet their customer's needs. You can't build much of a following by withholding products. However, there are those who use the mail to defraud. There are also firms that take orders before ordering the merchandise. Quite often they are nothing more than a mail drop, and they seldom meet their shipping requirements.

Also, sometimes a firm gets in trouble, and things are so bad they have to file bankruptcy, yet they still keep taking orders even though they know they will not be able to continue in operation. That means your claim for the unreceived order will have to go through the bankruptcy court, which can take years. Again, most firms are top drawer and you have nothing to worry about. However, when you do have a problem with a mail order firm, it's a nightmare to try and resolve.

Some outlets for assistance:

1. If you believe you are victim of fraud, the local Postmaster has forms to file a complaint with the Postal Inspectors. A time consuming process. The odds of getting your money back are slim, but you may help the perpetrators to spend a little time in jail and/or stop them from defrauding others.

2. If the complaint is local, file a complaint with the Better Business Bureau.

3. File a complaint with the State Attorney's Office in your state and the state where the company resides.

4. File a complaint with the Federal Trade Commission, Consumer Protection Bureau, Pennsylvania Ave. & Sixth St. NW, Washington, D.C. 20580-0000.

5. Most large cities have radio and TV station help lines. These can be quite effective, especially when dealing with a reputable firm that you have a dispute with. Unlike the outright fraud case, good companies respond to pressure from possible media coverage.

One tip that might stop you from having a problem in the first place is to not buy from a mail order firm you're not familiar with. There are companies springing up every day that are trying to get their share of the mail order boom. Wait until you receive a number of their catalogs over a period of months to make sure they are going to remain in business. Of course, you should ignore any mail order catalogs that offer bargains that are too good to be true.

Exercise caution when ordering through the mail. You're sending money, in some cases a lot of money, and/or your credit card number, to people you don't know. To people you can't see across the counter. People who do business hundreds or thousands of miles away from your front door. Companies that may have nothing more than a post office box for their office.

Mail order can be a great way to shop, and in most cases it is. But when things turn sour it can be a disaster. You have rights and agencies created to assist you. Use them.

COSTLY MISTAKES

In every endeavor it helps to have a realistic perspective. That's especially true in the world of personal finance.

While neither I nor anyone else should tell you what that perspective should be, you MUST have your own reality that guides your judgement. Basically there are two understandings that fit most cases. First, there is the " . . . life is a game, and money is the way of keeping score" group. At the other end of the spectrum is the " . . . money is green paper, and worthless until it is used as a means to buy something of tangible value" sect.

I find both points of view too extreme. First of all, since you can't take it with you, accumulating unusable wealth is "relative" in more ways than one. Secondly, anyone who has lived through the Depression, the subsequent number of recessions, and/or has ever had an unexpected financial or medical emergency, knows that some unused monetary backing offers an intangible but necessary security. In short, my perspective falls somewhere in between. Yours should too.

Regardless of your needs, it's imperative that you know what you expect from your money. Only then can you plan your attack. While I admit that some have made their fortune with little apparent effort, they are a product of percentage luck that dictates there will always be some winners who don't deserve the privilege. But, those odds are too long to be acceptable. No, as a rule, fortunes are made from hard work and dedication, which makes clear the requirement of setting your goals and outlining a plan to get where you want to go.

Having reached that understanding, there are some universal mistakes that most make along the way. They can be avoided. Knowing what they are and what corrective action to take can save you time, money and effort in your quest for financial security.

1. HAVING NO PLAN. Not to beat a dead horse, but it can't be said enough. You need a plan.

You wouldn't attempt to travel across country without a map, would you? Of course not. Yet, too many people try to get through life with no financial map, which is exactly why they fail. Your plan can and should change constantly in terms of specifics. Your goal(s) should tend to remain constant.

2. BECOMING MONETARILY INDECISIVE. So many of us promise to make more of an effort to supervise our money and then do just the opposite. That's not only sad, it's counterproductive.

We spend eight to ten hours a day, fifty weeks of the year, for forty or fifty years of our life on the job. And for what? Money, that's what! And then we spend little time making that money work the most efficiently. That's why people have bank accounts that produce so little interest income, and in times of high inflation actually lose money. That can only happen because someone got lazy. Remember, it's not just what money you make, it's what you make with the money you make that's important.

3. LOSING CONTROL OF YOUR FINANCES. It is amazing how many people, even some of the most affluent, lose control of their money. They can't tell you exactly how much they have, what their net worth is, what their earning assets are returning in terms of rate, where every dollar is, the present value of their real estate holdings, the worth of their life insurance cash surrender value, and so on.

Using our map analogy, how can you know where you're going if you don't know where you are? Take some time each month and review your finances. Have a budget and a current personal financial statement indicating an up-to-date net worth.

4. USING BAD ADVICE. My consulting business has made clear that too many rely on bad information to make their financial choices. There is the most obvious mistake of

the hot-tip from your brother-in-law. Then there is the more subtle one of your broker churning your account for his personal or house profit. To be successful you have to ignore bad advice. And the only way to know if it's bad advice is to take the time to investigate every commitment with your money.

Too often people come to me asking what this or that means *after* they've already invested their money. It's too late then. You must understand every nuance of each investment. If you don't, take a pass.

5. NOT SHOPPING. Financial investments and services are no different than grocery shopping or buying a new car. In those cases you'd shop around to find the best deal. But, when it comes to finances, many take the first thing available.

That's why people have bank checking accounts and cannot tell you what the bank charges per check or the minimum balance requirements are, how long before they receive credit for their deposits, etc. That's why most cannot tell you what rate their charge cards reflect and how those fees are arrived at. People, as a rule of thumb, don't shop financial services. Instead, for instance, they go to the nearest bank. You, in your financial lifetime, are going to spend a fortune in fees, service charges, interest, and the like. You cannot afford to forget that shopping your finances can save or make you tens of thousands of dollars.

6. NOT DIVERSIFYING. This needs no elaboration. If you put all your eggs in one basket, as the saying goes, you're going to get hurt.

Don't become so enamored with any financial opportunity, no matter how presently successful, that you fail to act on the universal constant that all financial opportunities are cyclical. The market goes up, the market goes down. Interest rates go up, interest rates go down. Real estate appreciates, real estate depreciates (in real terms). The point is, only a balanced portfolio works the majority of the time. If you don't diversify you will win, and then you'll lose, and in the process you'll give back all your winnings. That is an unacceptable result of your hard work and efforts.

If there is one strain of consistancy in all these mistakes, it is the misplaced value judgement that responsibility for one's financial success ends with earning a living. That is not true. It's only the beginning.

The bottomline says you must spend time and effort on your financial plan. If you're relying on your banker, your broker, your friends, your family, a crash course in buying real estate with no money down, or providence to be the catalyst that makes you financially secure, good luck. You'll need it.

PAYING WHOLESALE AT RETAIL STORES

Everyone likes a bargain, and most of us take advantage of wholesale opportunities when they're available. But many bargains are missed because the buyer didn't know a savings potential existed. Before making clear my direction, it must be noted that most goods have a mark-up of number plus one, which in plain English means, if the item costs $100 to reach the shelf it costs the consumer $200. Of course, there are numerous industries that have a mark-up far in excess of 100%. The more specialized, the higher the mark-up. Prescription drugs, for example, have an astronomical profit margin. On the other side of the coin, there are many industries that function on a minuscule margin, the banking industry for example. (I take banks to task whenever necessary, as they are often guilty of consumer abuse. However, on the subject of profit margin I fairly note that most industries couldn't survive on the margin of banks.)

In every retail environment, regardless of the exact margin, there is enough profit to allow the wise consumer negotiating room. That notwithstanding, the question remains, how do I save money when others can't or don't? Of course, as I always recommend, shop for bargains. With very little effort you can save 5 to 10 percent on most purchases. If you manage that average during your lifetime, your savings add up. This, in effect, is a consumer parallel to banking; i.e., a seemingly small percentage — 5 to 10% — when applied to a large volume — the purchases of a lifetime — amasses impressive savings. Unfortunately, most people look at each individual purchase and decide it's not worth the effort to try and save a few bucks. That misses the point, which is, during the average forty-year financial lifetime, the typical family spends approximately $1,600,000. A five percent reduction of that expense means a savings of $80,000. Ten percent saves $160,000. Imagine the return if those savings are invested. You're looking at enough money to comfortably retire. And this can be derived by doing nothing more than shopping smart, something everyone can and should do.

There is another, virtually unknown, savings method that will greatly enhance your ability to buy for less.

A substantial number of retail stores have their sales staff on a commission salary. That means the sticker or sales tag price on their merchandise is negotiable. The salesperson has leeway to negotiate your cost because part of the sales price includes his commission. If he lowers the price, he lowers his commission, but a lower percentage of a sizable commission is better than 100% of nothing. Each store has its own parameters for negotiated reductions in price. You must negotiate until you believe you've hit the floor of that parameter. Just because you're shopping at a major store in a large shopping mall doesn't mean the sales staff won't knock 5, 10, 15 percent off the cost of their top-of-the-line freezer. The secret is to politely demand a substantial reduction in cost and refuse to buy until you're successful. They're certainly not going to offer you a better deal if you're willing to pay retail. The same holds true with wholesale stores. In many cases they can offer you a much better bargain than their so-called lowest price. But, you have to ask.

Another easy method of cutting your costs, especially on major purchases, is to settle for almost new merchandise. In most instances the article would still retain warrantee, service rights, etc. All stores have orders that are returned almost immediately because the customer changed his mind. This also occurs with orders that are returned after a few months because the owner couldn't make the payments. In both instances, the returned merchandise is not supposed to be sold as new. What happens to the merchandise? It sits in the back waiting to be sold to a wholesaler who sells to a used or discount house. If you ask about returned merchandise, you can buy it before it leaves the back room. Savings of 50% are not uncommon.

This principle works with almost all purchases. In both cases, demanding a lower price or asking for returned merchandise, the aggressive consumer reaps the rewards.

It's OK to shop retail — as long as you pay wholesale.

LEASING: KNOW THE REAL COSTS

Leasing has, over the last ten years, become the choice of many. For example, there aren't too many businesses that don't have some sort of lease on some property.

Oftentimes, leases are contracted for the purpose of trying out an acquisition before being obligated to the high cost of an actual purchase. That's why so many manufacturers also become lessors (and set up their own lease company), as that lease option became another way to sell the product.

Then there was the possibility of the lease/buy that came into play. If you were satisfied with the product, you could turn your lease over into a straight purchase, usually at the end of the lease.

Probably more important than anything was the consideration of cash flow. For many companies this meant the difference between having necessary equipment or not. Oftentimes, a lease would cost the lessee nothing in terms of initial cash outlay. Monthly obligations were then kept to a known quantity through the lease payment. This was probably most important to smaller corporations.

Recently the lease has taken on a new twist. It has entered the retail market. Practically anything you and your family might consider purchasing is available through a lease. Many major retail companies not only have the lease option, they promote it heavily. The reason? Cars, for example, have become too expensive. A lease tends to mute that fact from the public. It's much easier to sell an overpriced $20,000.00 piece of plastic, tin, and rubber that masquerades as Detroit's answer to an automobile if you talk in terms of lease payments. Lease payments sound so harmless. There is no focus, as there is with a purchase, on the total cost of the car, the interest, the insurance, etc. There is just that one simple monthly payment. And you don't even own the car! At the end of the lease you just turn back the car and it's the lessor's problem. It doesn't sound too bad, but of course, like most repackaging, it's dangerous.

You must exercise caution with any financial transaction that is a market repackaging. This is true when you deal with your bank, your car dealer, your broker, etc. Repackaging seldom offers anything to the consumer except additional hidden costs.

Most business people are financially educated enough to decipher a lease. The same cannot be said by most who enter into a retail lease. That doesn't mean the business is smarter than a consumer (quite the contrary actually). It simply means that a business probably employs legal counsel who can translate the lease into terms management can understand. Also, a business may make a lease decision for completely different reasons than a consumer would. Certainly there are times when a lease makes sense in a business environment.

Let's review some important points to consider in any lease. These are minimum requirements, as a lease mistake can cost you more money, time and grief than you can possibly imagine. Like most financial transactions, a lease deserves excessive preventive maintenance.

1. THE TRUE COST OF THE LEASE. This includes the monthly payment amount, the total repaid over the term of the lease, the total due (if any) at the end of the lease, etc. Overlook nothing. What is the disposition of the property at the end of the lease? Is it yours, or do you owe another substantial payment before title transfers?

The important thing here is to arrive at a real bottom-line cost. A lease can look extremely attractive until you put a pencil to it. Your actual cost could be far in excess of normal traditional financing.

2. THE UP-FRONT PAYMENT. Many leases have installation or set-up costs. Those figures are then added to the lease, which is something most lessees don't notice. Find out what these fees are, their exact costs, and their disposi-

tion. If you don't pay attention, you can be fee'd to death without knowing it. Ask questions and make sure everything, in this regard, is spelled out in the contract.

3. SECURITY DEPOSITS. Many lessors require a security deposit. If your lease has this provision make sure you understand it. Don't automatically assume you will receive the security deposit back at the end of the lease, because often times a security deposit is nothing more than a cleverly disguised non-refundable fee.

Also, you should receive interest on your security deposit. Check the lease. If not, you're being abused.

4. ADDITIONAL CHARGES. Many leases have substantial penalty costs. Ascertain exactly what they are before you find out the hard way. A few considerations: what is the charge for a late payment, the charge for use over the maximum use term, the cost of lease cancellation, etc.

Most leases have more contingencies than the normal person could possibly understand or consider. These additional charges tend to get lost in the shuffle. Remember, that lease agreement was designed by lawyers who work for the lessor. It is not designed so you can understand it, nor for your protection. The odds are, that lease will have some hidden costs that will bring you to your knees if the lease relationship turns sour. Again, you can't be too cautious.

5. MAINTENANCE COSTS. Who's responsible for what costs? Is your warranty valid if you use a lease as opposed to a straight purchase? Who pays for routine maintenance? Usually the consumer is told, in the selling process, that one of the good things about a lease is that they don't have to worry about maintenance. That sounds good, but in many cases it's only partly true. The consumer has to pay for most maintenance regardless of what the salesman said. Check the fine print!

One additional note. What happens if, in this case, the car is in the shop for a month? Do they provide a replacement? Do you get credit on your lease? If these questions aren't spelled out, include them on the lease as an addendum.

6. WHO'S RESPONSIBLE FOR THE INSURANCE? More often than not it's the lessee, which means you have another substantial cost not exactly spelled out.

There is the possibility that the lessor will acquire the insurance, but you are required to pay for it. The problem here is, many times the company that will be insuring the equipment is another company that belongs to the lessor. You will never know that, which is a disclosure I believe you are entitled to. The problem is further enhanced as their premium is seldom competitive, since there is a captive market.

It may sound to some that I am overstating our case. I'm not. A retail lease is not understood by too many who enter into such an agreement. They end up paying far more than necessary, simply because they didn't understand the intent of the document. That being, to take as much of your money as possible.

It would be prudent to allow your accountant to review any lease you are considering, as the tax considerations have recently changed dramatically. Also, you may have special financial considerations that may have added bearing on a lease, which is something else your accountant can review with you.

I believe in solving problems before the fact. Financial preventive maintenance is always important, but probably acute in a lease arrangement. If you have questions or problems with the boilerplate lease the lessor makes available, negotiate! If they won't, you may wish to shop elsewhere, as, if you have trouble at this point, imagine the trouble you're going to have when there really is a problem.

Leases, while having some advantages for some people, can often be dangerous and costly.

SAVING YOUR MEDICAL DOLLAR

Last year the cost of medical care in this country was an astounding 435 billion dollars. That's equal to more than $1,700.00 for every man, woman, and child in America. Many experts in the field admit that perhaps 50% of medical expenses are for treatment not needed. Regardless, at these prices it pays to make good use of your medical dollar.

There are some things you can do to limit your costs:

1. CONSIDER TAKING A MEDICAL SELF-HELP HEALTH CARE CLASS. Offered by most local hospitals and the Red Cross, these classes can give you an important insight into medical problems and treatments. You'll find, once you understand them, most general illnesses are just going to take time and they'll go away. The other important side of the coin is, the more knowledge you have, the quicker you'll seek help when it is actually necessary.

2. MAINTAIN A MEDICAL JOURNAL FOR EVERY MEMBER OF YOUR FAMILY. List all illnesses, operations, doctor's visits, shots, etc. Write down the major medical histories of your immediate relatives also. Many medical problems are passed on through generations, so one of the first things a doctor does in serious health matters is ask questions about your father, mother, and grandparents. It will save time and money if you have that information at your immediate disposal.

Solving many serious medical problems is like solving a mystery and anything you can give the doctor to assist him or her will help.

3. ASK YOUR LOCAL HOSPITAL FOR A COPY OF THE BOOKLET ENTITLED "PATIENTS BILL OF RIGHTS." You need to know all of your options.

4. TAKE CARE OF YOURSELF. Drugs, alcohol, smoking, and the like are going to do you damage, costly damage.

There is no reason to push your luck. An exercise program is an excellent idea if you don't overdo it.

If you have to visit the doctor, there are some things you can do that will help him help you:

1. BEFORE GOING TO A DOCTOR'S OFFICE DETERMINE THAT THE VISIT IS NEEDED. It is estimated that as many as 70% of all the patients in a doctor's waiting room don't need to be there.

Buy a reputable medical reference book, so you have at least limited understanding of your problem. It will help you analyze the doctor's actions.

2. WRITE DOWN ALL YOUR QUESTIONS YOU WANT TO ASK THE DOCTOR. There's nothing worse than getting home and realizing you forgot to ask numerous questions you are concerned about. The best way to ensure this doesn't happen is write your inquiries down and don't let the doctor leave the room until he answers them to your satisfaction.

3. TELL THE DOCTOR ALL HE NEEDS TO KNOW. For instance, keeping an embarrassing aspect of a problem to yourself means the doctor's ability to help is limited.

4. ASK "WHY" EVERY TIME YOU DON'T UNDERSTAND SOMETHING. A positive mental attitude affects your healing, and it's much easier to have that positive outlook if you believe in the doctor's actions. You need to know what is being done and for what reason.

5. IF YOU NEED SURGERY, GET A SECOND OPINION. No reputable doctor will be offended by that request.

Understand, many believe that as many as 50% of all operations are unnecessary! Add to that the fact that all surgery, no matter how minor, involves risk, substantial risk. The bottomline says you have to know your surgery is required.

6. IF SURGERY IS NEEDED, SEE IF IT CAN BE DONE ON AN OUTPATIENT BASIS. The surgery can be

just as safe and efficient in this form, while saving substantial costs.

7. NEVER BE AFRAID TO ASK HOW MUCH ANY TREATMENT IS GOING TO COST. This is seldom done and causes many to be shocked when they receive their bill from the doctor, hospital, additional physicians, consultants, etc.

I am not suggesting that you plan on bargaining with the doctor, just that you know your costs before you owe the bill.

8. PROBABLY MOST IMPORTANT IS TAKING CONTROL OF YOUR MEDICAL TREATMENT. The doctor works for you and should answer your questions, offer you respect, be sympathetic, and professional.

As you know, many doctors believe they are a form of deity and as such needn't be bothered by us mere mortals. That's why patients have to wait hours, can't get answers in the hospital, are taking prescription drugs without knowing the side effects, and so on.

If necessary, you must demand that you are included in the thought process that is supposed to heal you. If the doctor won't make time for your concerns, find a doctor who will.

There are many aspects of this problem that aren't mentioned here, but being all-inclusive isn't my objective. What is important is that you start asking questions and demanding answers. Realize that you control a goodly portion of the doctor/patient relationship. DON'T BE INTIMIDATED.

Start a preventive maintenance health program, and don't run to the doctor every time you catch cold. The fact is, DOCTORS CURE VERY FEW THINGS. What they do is give you medicine to mute your symptoms until nature does its work.

You can probably safely save 50% of the cost you're now spending on health care. If you've got a good insurance plan that's great, but you should take additional monetary precautions. Even good insurance plans will cost you 20% of the total bill. In many cases, that can add up to thousands, or tens of thousands of dollars. In New York City for example, a hospital bed can cost $1,200 per day. Everything else, of course, is extra. So you can see, even with insurance, you should try and limit your costs. Then too, many medical treatments are not covered by certain policies, and/or the deductible may be quite high. The point is, insurance or not, you cannot afford to ignore any chance to lower your medical costs.

If you need medical help, seek it immediately. Money can be replaced, your health can't. However, don't forget the statistics as expressed by medical professionals. AT LEAST HALF THE MEDICAL TREATMENT BEING PAID FOR EVERY DAY IS NOT NECESSARY.

BILLING PROBLEMS?

Have you ever had a billing problem? If you have, you know what a nightmare it is. Especially now that computers have taken over. Once an erroneous amount is charged to your account, it's almost impossible to get things corrected. And it's not only the dollar amount in question that's going to give you fits. Your credit rating with that store and/or others will more than likely be negatively affected.

You may end up spending months trying to resolve matters. You will spend time, money, and effort and even if you're lucky and manage to get the store, credit card company, bank, etc., to make the appropriate adjustment, you will find the entire experience very unsatisfying.

Well, take heart. There is an answer to the runaround that clerks, managers, and corporate officers, will give you. It's called "Fair Credit Billing", an addition to the Federal Truth and Lending Law. You have many rights and the entity extending credit has many obligations. Unfortunately, not many consumers are aware of their rights which allows for continual customer abuse.

What constitutes a billing error? A billing error is any charge:

1. NOT MADE BY, OR AUTHORIZED BY YOU.

2. NOT CLEARLY IDENTIFIED. Different dates, amounts, etc., that you know are incorrect.

3. FOR ITEMS NOT DELIVERED OR NOT DE-LIVERED AS AGREED.

Billing errors also include:

1. FAILURE TO CREDIT YOUR ACCOUNT.

2. ACCOUNTING MISTAKES.

3. MAILING YOUR STATEMENT TO AN IM-
PROPER ADDRESS if you properly notified the
creditor 10 days prior to mail date.

4. ITEMS IN DISPUTE. Those items on the bill
that you properly requested an explanation for but
haven't received a corresponding reply.

If you think a billing error has occurred, you should follow these steps:

1. NOTIFY THE CREDITOR IN WRITING WITHIN 60
DAYS AFTER THE BILL WAS MAILED. Explain the error,
why you believe it's an error, and the amount of the error. Be
sure to include your name and address and your account
number.

2. YOU ARE NOT REQUIRED TO MAKE PAYMENTS
ON DISPUTED AMOUNTS WHILE YOU ARE WAITING
FOR AN ANSWER. Normal payments, if necessary, are re-
quired on those amounts not in dispute.

3. THE CREDITOR MUST RESPOND WITHIN 30
DAYS unless they make the appropriate correction. If they
believe the amount is correct as stated, they have to tell you
why they believe so within 90 days.

4. IF THE CREDITOR MADE A MISTAKE, YOU DO
NOT HAVE TO PAY ANY FINANCE CHARGES ON THAT
AMOUNT.

5. IF THEY DO NOT BELIEVE THERE IS AN ERROR,
YOU MUST EITHER TAKE LEGAL ACTION — A GOOD
CASE FOR SMALL CLAIMS COURT — OR ACCEPT
THEIR DECISION.

What about your credit rating? No creditor can give out
negative information regarding a charge presently in dispute. They cannot threaten to damage your credit rating.

However, if they have responded following the law, they
can then, after declining to correct the item in dispute, report you as delinquent. They can even start collection proce-

dures if you refuse to pay. However, and this is important, if they do report the non-payment, they must also report that the item is in dispute. Further, they have to furnish you in writing a list (name and address) of all those to whom they made reports. Lastly, once the matter is settled, they must then re-report the outcome to all those they contacted or made information available.

It must be mentioned that the creditor can charge the disputed amount against your credit line, even during the dispute.

You should also know that you may withhold payment on items purchased with a credit card that are not acceptable because they are defective. This right is only applicable if you have made a reasonable effort to correct the problem with the supplier or simply returned the merchandise.

There are limitations here which may make you reconsider long distance purchases over the phone or through the mails. The original purchase must be over $50.00, and the sale must have taken place in your state or within 100 miles of your current address.

Any creditor who fails to meet their obligations as outlined in the Fair Credit Billing section of the Truth and Lending Law forfeits the amount of the disputed item and up to $50.00 of finance charges EVEN IF NO ERROR ACTUALLY EXISTED!

As an individual, you may sue for dollar amount damages, plus twice the amount of finance charges (not less than $100.00 or more than $1,000.00). Class action suits are also permissible.

Creditors must give you a copy of your Fair Credit Billing Rights when you open your account. At least twice annually they must do so again — some companies include same on the monthly billing statements.

If you want a free copy of the Fair Credit Bill you may write the:

Director
Office of Consumer Affairs
F.D.I.C.
Washington, D.C. 20429

Fair Credit Billing is one of those areas where the consumer has rights but seldom uses them to his or her advantage. When disputes arise, most people, after spending hours, days, or weeks, trying to right things, give up. All that does is cost you money, and encourage the offending company to continue to exploit. Millions of dollars are lost every year because consumers failed to understand their rights and the creditor's obligations.

Don't underestimate the importance of this subject. If you end up paying an erroneous $50.00 dispute, that's the equivalent of losing a month's worth of 10% interest on $6,000.00.

Worth fighting for? You bet it is.

RESOLVING COMPLAINTS

It is becoming more and more difficult to find services that are worth the money. It seems that fewer professionals believe in the traditional American work ethic, which is why the consumer is spending more for less. In short, your chances of being dissatisfied with someone you have hired for financial or personal matters has increased dramatically. It will help if you're prepared for this almost certain eventuality.

First, regardless of the circumstances, if you're paying for a service, make sure you keep all documentation referencing the transaction(s). Why? Because you should enter the relationship assuming there will be problems down the line. It is much easier on you and your finances if you're prepared.

Next, assuming the worst comes to pass, try and resolve matters directly. If that becomes impossible, go over the individual's head and see their supervisor and/or boss if that's possible.

Here are other options if things are still unresolved:

1. If your difficulty is with an attorney, you may file a complaint with your local bar association. My experience indicates that any time one attorney investigates another the consumer suffers, which is why you shouldn't expect an unbiased result for your effort.

If that's the case, or if your complaint is of a more serious nature, you may wish to contact the American Bar Association, 750 N. Lake Shore Drive, Chicago, IL 60611. Phone 1-312-988-5158.

If your problem is related to your attorney's fees and nothing more, the local bar association can offer fee arbitration to resolve matters.

Again, lawyers reviewing the conduct of other lawyers is not my idea of objectivity, so I have to offer that, perhaps more than any other professional industry, winning a dispute with a lawyer is difficult. Which is why I remind you that you can sue your lawyer for malpractice. Finding a good attorney to file such a suit is becoming easier all the time. To be safe, however, I recommend a malpractice specialist, and someone not in your local area.

2. If your complaint is against your tax accountant, you should contact the Internal Revenue Service, the Better Business Bureau, and your state's consumer affairs office.

If your tax preparer is a Certified Public Accountant contact your state's Board of Certified Accounts.

Accountants are a lot like lawyers in that they believe they are dealing with an uneducated public and therefore they have nothing to fear no matter how substandard their work. Don't be intimidated.

3. If your complaint is with a real estate agent or office, register a protest with The National Association of Realtors, 777 14th St., NW, Washington, DC 20005. Phone 1-202-383-1000. Here too you have one industry professional investigating another, so have realistic expectations.

Of course, real estate offices and agents have to be licensed to do business in your state, so you can file a complaint with the State Real Estate Commission or the Department of Real Estate. Don't forget the Better Business Bureau and the state consumer affairs office.

4. If your complaint is with a financial planner, your direct line of communication is less defined because the industry is so new.

While there are no licensing requirements per se, you can register a complaint with the International

Association of Financial Planning, 2 Concourse Parkway, Suite 800, Atlanta, GA 30328. Phone 1-800-241-2148. Or, the Institute of Certified Financial Planners, 3443 S. Galena, Suite 190, Denver, CO 80231. Phone 1-303-751-7600.

A letter to the state consumer affairs office and the Better Business Bureau would also be appropriate.

If your financial planner is a stockbroker, contact the Securities and Exchange Commission, 450 Fifth St. NW, Washington, DC 20001. Phone 1-202-272-2650.

If your complaint is with an insurance agent, contact your state's Department of Insurance and the National Association of Insurance Commissioners, 1125 Grand Ave., Kansas City, MO 64106. Phone 1-414-784-9540. Or, the National Association of Professional Insurance Agents, 400 N. Washington St., Alexandria, VA 22314. Phone 1-703-836-9340.

Regardless of the problem and/or who you're having it with, never forget your option of Small Claims Court. If your suit would fall below the state minimum, you can find direct and simple justice at a most reasonable cost. If you're not familiar with small claims, ask the clerk for their free booklet outlining the system and how to make it work.

There are also a number of fine inexpensive reference books on Small Claims Court. Ask at your bookstore. One that I have found useful is, *Everybody's Guide to Small Claims Court*, by Ralph Warner (Nolo Press, P.O. Box 544, Occidental, CA 95465).

Knowing how to use Small Claims Court is important, as almost all your legal problems, complaints, etc., can be solved through this forum. And, since many states don't allow lawyers in Small Claims Court, your chances of a fair hearing are greatly enhanced.

Lastly, don't overlook your option of arbitration. This presents an excellent, cost-efficient way of resolving almost any matter. Most arbitration panels are made up of experts in their field, and many won't allow lawyers in the process.

Perhaps the worst part of the lack of financial professionalism is that, as consumers, we have come to accept the fact that we are paying more for less every day. The system is too huge and complex for us to fight, so we pay the outrageous bills and chalk it up to experience. Of course, we're no closer to resolving our problem; in fact, we may now have more problems than we had before we contacted our lawyer, financial planner, real estate agent, or tax accountant, but what can we do?

Plenty. My consulting experience makes it clear that an aggressive consumer almost always wins a viable case. Yes, it takes time and effort, but those who succeed are repaid on many levels. Don't waste your hard-earned money. Never let a professional present you with a bill for anything other than professional service.

DON'T BUY THAT SERVICE CONTRACT

If you've purchased a major appliance recently, you know that part of the total sales effort is spent trying to convince buyers that they need an extended warranty via a service contract. While most warranties available with the purchase are for ninety days, for both parts and labor, a service contract extends that period for one year. Multiple year contracts are occasionally offered. Regardless, seldom does the extended term continue beyond two or three years.

Terms of the service contracts vary from firm to firm. Some, the most expensive, cover all parts and labor. More commonly, labor is covered as well as a few specific parts. Non-covered parts are extra. In some instances, there is a deductible of $X. In others, you have to follow a prescribed sequence of preventive maintenance for the warranty to be in effect. Make one small error and you've lost your coverage. Terms are quite varied as you can see. It is fair to say, however, that most are designed to offer little actual benefit.

As you might imagine, the real benefit is not to the consumer, but rather to the warrantee firm and the store where you bought the appliance. The warrantee firm profits because they have little chance of having to pay on the contract. The store profits from the approximate 40% kickback they get for selling the service contract (for example, if the service contract is for two years at $200.00, the store makes an immediate $80.00). The consumer? The odds are overwhelmingly against the contract even breaking even on cost. In almost all cases it's a direct loss. Or, if it helps to look at it another way, you substantially increased the true cost of the appliance. On a big appliance, like a freezer, these tricks may mean an added expense of one to three hundred dollars — which could increase the freezer's cost by ten to forty percent.

The tip-off that service contracts are a bad, bad buy is rather obvious in that they are only offered for a short period of time. For instance, when you purchase a refrigerator, you expect it to last approximately eight to ten years. Yet, the service contract offered is only for one to two years. There is an obvious reason for the term. The warrantee firm wants no part of your appliance after the time the firm believes it might actually break down. They have spent time, money, and effort determining exactly when the appliance becomes a liability. And shortly before that is the point where your contract is no longer valid.

While no actual figures are available (since warrantee firms, as well as manufacturers and appliance outlets refuse to make the information public), it is estimated that only three percent of service contracts ever receive any benefit.

Service contracts are so profitable that in many stores the profit margin on service is greater than on the actual sale of the appliance. If extended warranties actually offered any consumer benefit, the warrantee company could not afford a 40% fee to the outlet for selling the contract. Of course, many larger stores have their own warrantee subsidiary that offers service contracts. Their profit potential is 100%.

Consumers should be interested in the paradox of service contracts. When you buy an appliance, the salesman advises you to buy their brand because it's dependable, and " . . . it will last a lifetime". Yet immediately after the sale he, or a phone solicitor, tells you, via their extended warranty sales pitch, that the product is substandard and you should buy insurance because it probably won't last more than a year or two. Of course, that's not the case, as most major appliances from national firms last a long time. For example, on average, a color TV lasts eight years, air conditioners ten, washers and dryers eleven, refrigerators sixteen, and furnaces twenty. Only a fraction of these will have any problem before half of their life span elapses. Sadly, the service contract is only valid during the time when the facts say the appliance is least likely to have problems. That's what this issue is all about. Offering a high priced "service" that offers little.

To be fair, I have to bring to your attention those rare instances when a service contract may be worthy of consideration. For example, if you live in a Southern climate, you may wish to buy an extended warranty for a freezer because, since it will be on constantly, it probably won't last as long as the average. Under these circumstances you may beat the odds of collecting.

But, I have to remind you, when you buy a service contract you are betting that the new appliance you just purchased, for a great deal of money, is a piece of junk —because, if it needs repair within the limited time period offered by the extended warranty, it's exactly that. If you and the salesman are that unsure of the appliance's reliability, buy another brand!

Lastly, there is what is referred to as the manufacturer's ninety day rule, which states: If it hasn't broken within 90 days, it will probably meet the average life span for that type of appliance. That's the standard used by appliance professionals. It means, if you use the appliance normally during the standard 90 day warranty period (I recommend constant, harder use to make flaws immediately apparent), you are fairly secure that the appliance will meet your needs without the cost of a service contract. Appliance manufacturers believe and base business decisions on that fact — why should you, by buying a service contract, doubt them. It's unfortunate that consumers have come to believe that they have to pay extra for a manufacturer to stand behind their product. We have become accustomed to paying more for less, which is why service contracts came into being. They are playing on our fears. Again, most major appliances, while grossly overpriced, are made well enough to last far in excess of the limited service contract term.

For a free bulletin on service contracts, write the Federal Trade Commission, Public Reference Branch, Room 130, Washington, DC 20580. Ask for *Facts for Consumers*. Their bulletin is designed to explain what to look for when buying a service contract. If you read it with my point of view in mind, it substantiates my position. I draw it to your attention for that purpose and for those who, as mentioned above, might have unique circumstances that may make a service contract worthy of consideration.

YOU MAY BE OWED MONEY

Not many people are aware of unclaimed money that may be theirs. This abandoned property is in the control of state governments. In most instances, it is in the form of cash. The state receives it after a financial institution, insurance company, or corporation can no longer locate the rightful owner. This happens for many reasons. For instance: a bank can't locate a customer who has moved and forgotten a savings account, or an insurance company didn't pay a widow a benefit because she died not knowing her husband had such a policy. Even paid, unused airline tickets can become abandoned property. The time requirement for property to be turned in to the state is normally between two and seven years, depending on individual state law.

What are the chances that some of the money transferred to state control belongs to you? One out of ten families are owed money they don't know about. New York alone has over six million names on its abandoned property list.

And how much money is involved? In total, well over a half billion dollars. Most individual claims are small, but there are cases where claimants received almost a million dollars each. Lesser payments of twenty, thirty, or forty thousand dollars are not that uncommon.

States keep this money forever under the supposition that the owners, or their heirs, will someday be found. In effect, the state assumes the property as a custodian or trustee. Consequently, there is no time limitation involved regarding legitimate claims.

The first thing you have to do to make a claim is call the state to find out if you are owed money. Call your state's Information Office (usually located at the capitol) or its Information Directory and ask for the name, address, and phone number of the office your state has assigned the responsibility of abandoned property. In most states that will be a department or division of the State Treasury Office, Division of

Revenue, Department of Financial Institutions, or Office of the Treasurer. Locate this office in every state where you and your relatives have lived, owned property, gone to college, or may have done business. This may be time-consuming if done correctly, but it's worth being thorough. States are helpful in this process, so don't be afraid to ask for assistance if you have questions or don't understand their directions. Some states are more helpful than others. For example, some offices will do all this research work for you over the phone. Others require written notice.

When checking with the state office, you have to remember to offer every conceivable possibility. Give them every name, first, middle, and last that might be related. Give maiden names where appropriate. Don't forget children's names, as many times a savings account was opened in the name of a child and then forgotten. Give social security numbers, former addresses, etc. When researching your possible ownership of funds, go back as far as your parents, grandparents, great grandparents. If money in state control belonged to them, it now belongs to you, their descendants. An important point: the state office can only be as good as the information you give them. If your deceased mother had an account or money that was in her maiden name, but you only give her married name, you will never be informed of the account. This is one of those cases where overkill is appropriate, so, once again, I urge you to be thorough. Check with other relatives to see if they have information regarding distant relatives you should include in your search.

The best, most time-efficient method is to make up a listing of all that information and make copies to send to every applicable state office.

A response from most states takes approximately a month. They will respond regardless of the answer. If it is yours, you will be given information on how you may claim the money. The actual process of collecting is surprisingly simple in most cases. Usually it requires nothing more than positive identification if the money was in your name, and confirmation/proof of the relationship if the money belonged

to a relative. Again, the states are usually quite accommo-
dating and willing to help. While not wishing to denigrate
their assistance, you should know that the state will only return the monies sent to them, they do not pay interest regardless of how long they have had the funds. That is to say,
if a bank sent them five hundred dollars fifteen years ago,
all they will send to the rightful owner is five hundred dollars. Their profit comes from investing the funds in their
abandoned property account. The interest earned goes to the
general revenue fund.

Some people, for a variety of reasons, have difficulty
with the concept of looking for unclaimed abandoned property. Perhaps it doesn't feel right to them. That shouldn't be
the case. If you lost a thousand dollars, you'd look for it. It's
no different if your grandparents did some twenty years ago.
In each case the money belongs to you. Certainly the state
doesn't deserve it.

Because of the odds involved in the process, and the
amount of money in abandoned property accounts, many of
you will be successful in your search. A few of you will find
tens of thousands of dollars, maybe more.

SAVINGS ON YOUR PHONE BILL

Since deregulation, phone companies have carried on an active campaign to garner or retain your service. That competition, the motivating and deciding factor of deregulation approval, would, under normal circumstances, drive the cost of telephone service downward. That's what free market competition is all about. But lower costs haven't materialized. Has your phone bill gone down? To the contrary, it's probably gone up, substantially up. Once again, a supposedly consumer beneficial law has had the opposite effect.

There is nothing we can do about this event, so I will confine my concerns to actions you can take to lower your phone bill in this newly competitive, yet costly, environment. And the best place to start is reviewing your present services, as there are probably at least a few you don't really need.

1. CALL WAITING. This service, particularly aggravating when you're put on hold by someone who has called you, allows the subscriber to know if they have another call while their line is in use. Its only conceivable merit would be an emergency, but even that isn't applicable as, if necessary, an operator will break into a conversation, at no charge, to inform you of an emergency call. Savings: $30.00 per year.

2. CALL FORWARDING. You would have to be extremely busy and travel a lot to make this cost-effective. If you're going to be out and expect a call, why not contact the person prior to leaving and give them the number where you can be reached? Or, buy a phone answering machine and leave the number on your message. Granted the machine costs money, but they're fairly inexpensive now and once purchased don't generate a monthly bill. Savings: $30.00 per year.

3. SPEED DIALING. Are you really so busy that dialing two numbers instead of seven makes a difference in your life? I doubt it. However, if you're one of the few who require the service, a much cheaper one-time expense is to buy a

phone that offers programmable one-touch dialing. Savings: $30.00 per year.

4. THREE-WAY CALLS. This has a business application that might pay for itself or it might be a business necessity. However, at your home, at best it may be used once or twice a year on holidays. Savings: $30.00 per year.

5. UNLISTED NUMBER. If you have a personal reason for an unlisted number, it is well worth the cost. But, if you have an unlisted number because you think it will protect you from phone solicitors you're mistaken. There are many ways telemarketing companies can get your number. Then too, the more sophisticated sales call programs dial by selecting random numbers in a predetermined market area. Your chances of being bothered are not demonstrably diminished by having an unlisted number. Savings $17.00 per year.

6. MAINTENANCE AGREEMENTS. Your local phone company offers an inside wiring maintenance agreement for a fee of approximately $1.00 to $2.75 per month. That sounds reasonable, but ask yourself, when's the last time such service was required? Not one person I know has ever had an inside residential wiring problem. If one does occur, the phone company will repair the difficulty on a per hour basis. Savings: Up to $33.00 per year.

It should be noted that some companies offer the above mentioned services as a package; i.e., you can lower the per service cost if you'll take a minimum of three. But, saving a portion of an expense you probably should avoid in total isn't truly a savings.

There are a number of other things you can do to lower your phone costs.

1. UNDERSTAND THE LONG DISTANCE SCHEDULE. Most know it's cheaper to call at certain times of the day and week, but don't know exactly when those times are.

Or, even if they do, they seldom arrange their phone schedule to take advantage of the savings. Without elaborating
beyond necessity, all you have to remember is that an AT&T
long distance call after 5 P.M. your time, Monday through
Friday, saves approximately 30%. The same call after 11
P.M. (to 8 A.M.) your time, Monday through Friday, all day
Saturday and until 5 P.M. on Sunday, saves approximately
50% on that bill.

    With little forethought, you can organize your calls and
reduce your expense. That's especially true for those in the
East. They can dial after 5 P.M. and still be calling other
sections of the country during business hours.

    2. GET A LONG DISTANCE CARD. Operator-assisted
calls are the most expensive. A long distance card, available
on request, will eliminate the need for operator assistance
when you're not at home and must place a long distance call.
On average, a card will save at least $1.00 per call.

    3. USE 800 SERVICE. Almost every major company has
an 800 phone line to their main office. Before using your
quarter, call 1-800-555-1212 and see if the company you
want to talk to provides such service. If so, the call is free.
The savings can be huge.

    4. COMPARISON SHOP. While cost shouldn't be the
overriding consideration for the choice of a carrier, you certainly should explore what others offer. Like service doesn't
cost the same with each company. There is money to be
saved. Check every phone company. An excellent, easily understood test is to send them your present bill and ask what
their charges would have been. The best buy will be obvious.

    The problem with phone service is that it gets little con-
sumer consideration. Most people follow the advice of their
phone company representative, whose job is to sell as many
services as possible. Then too, as phone companies always
talk in terms of charges per month, the costs sound reasonable. After all, what's another $2.50? Of course, charges add
up.

With very little effort and the cancellation of a few worthless services, the average family can save a minimum $15.00 per month. Hardly sounds worth the effort does it? Before you decide, let's deposit that money into a savings/investment plan because, as I always say, it's not just the savings but what you do with the savings that counts. A $15.00 per month savings plan at 10% compounded interest over the span of a forty year financial lifetime gives a balance of $94,861.19.

Projections of the better use of savings are important. That's why I keep bringing the principle to your attention. It's a monetary mind-set that allows one to maximize their use of money. Your phone costs are a perfect example of how an expense that appears too small to be concerned with can, when looked at from a different perspective, be well worth every effort to lower.

FEDERAL SURPLUS PROPERTY SALES

The Federal surplus property sales program is authorized by the Federal Property and Administrative Services Act of 1949. It allows individuals or businesses to purchase property that the government has declared it no longer has use for... cars, trucks, business supplies, construction equipment, typewriters, medical equipment, and furniture, just to name a few.

As you can image, the property for sale can be of varying quality. Some is excellent, some needs repairs, and some isn't worth any price. If you're interested, make sure you carefully inspect any item you have an interest in, as, once you buy it, it's yours — there are no refunds at a government surplus sale.

The two major agencies that sell surplus to the public are the Department of Defense (DOD) and the Government Service Administration (GSA). Since the GSA has the most to offer the general public, you may find pursuing their offers the most useful.

All sales are made in one of the following three manners:

1. AUCTION. These sales are conducted with an auctioneer. Property is offered item by item with all bids being verbal.

2. SPOT BID. A varying method of auctioning. Merchandise is offered item by item, but bids are made through written offer.

3. SEALED BID. The agency making the sale offers a written bidding form to prospective buyers through an Invitation for Bids (IFB). The form describes the property, explains where and when the property can be inspected, and then gives directions on how to make a bid if so desired. On the date of the sale, all previously submitted sealed bids are opened publicly, with the highest bidders winning specific property.

There are differing conditions of the sales. You should know them before making an offer:

1. GENERAL CONDITIONS. All surplus property is sold under the guidelines outlined under the General Sales Terms & Conditions (Form 114C). Ask for a copy at the nearest GSA Customer Service Bureau.

2. SPECIAL CONDITIONS. Certain property, for a variety of reasons, is sold subject to special conditions. If there are such conditions on a sale, you will be offered a notice making clear the nuances.

3. AWARDS. If the highest bid meets the minimum set by the DOD or GSA for that specific merchandise, the auction is complete. If bids fall below the minimum, the property will be removed from the auction and offered at a later date.

4. PAYMENT AND REMOVAL. Winning bidders must pay for their property with cash, money order, traveler's checks, government check, cashier's check, or certain letters of credit. Nothing can be removed unless paid for in full. Your winning bid can be lost if you fail to have the means to pay immediately.

Information regarding government surplus sales can be obtained through the following GSA regional Customer Service Bureaus:

1.   NATIONAL CAPITAL REGION
       (Washington, DC)

       7th and D Streets, SW
       Washington, DC 20407

2. REGION 1
   (Connecticut, Maine, Massachusetts, New Hamp-
   shire, Rhode Island, & Vermont)

   Post Office & Courthouse
   Boston, MA 02109

3. REGION 2
   (New Jersey, New York)

   26 Federal Plaza
   New York, NY 10278

4. REGION 3
   Delaware, Maryland, Virginia, Pennsylvania & West
   Virginia)

   Ninth & Market Streets
   Philadelphia, PA 19107

5. REGION 4
   (Alabama, Florida, Georgia, Kentucky, Mississippi,
   North Carolina, South Carolina, & Tennessee)

   75 Spring St., SW
   Atlanta, GA 30303

6. REGION 5
   (Illinois, Indiana, Michigan, Minnesota, Ohio, & Wis-
   consin)

   230 S. Dearborn St.
   Chicago, IL 60604

7. REGION 6
   (Iowa, Kansas, Missouri, & Nebraska)

   1500 E. Bannister Rd.
   Kansas City, MO 64131

8. REGION 7

(Arkansas, Louisiana, New Mexico, Oklahoma, & Texas)

819 Taylor St.
Fort Worth, TX 76102

9. REGION 8

(Colorado, Montana, North Dakota, South Dakota, Utah, & Wyoming)

Bldg. 41 — Denver Federal Center
Denver, CO 80225

10. REGION 9

(Arizona, California, Hawaii & Nevada)

525 Market St.
San Francisco, CA 94105

11. REGION 10

(Alaska, Idaho, Oregon & Washington)

GSA Center
Auburn, WA 98002

For information regarding DOD sales, write to Defense Reutilization and Marketing Service, Federal Center, P.O. Box 1370, Battle Creek, Michigan 49016.

For general information regarding government surplus sales (such as confiscated property acquired with the profits from illegal drug activity), subscribe to *The Commerce Business Daily*, which is available by writing the Superintendent of Documents, Government Printing Office, Washington, DC 20402. Many libraries and/or Chamber of Commerce offices have copies available if you wish to save the subscription fee.

There are many excellent buys through government surplus auctions (cars, boats, and pick-up trucks have sold for as little as $100). They have exceptional merit if you are looking for commercial or industrial property. For instance, farm tractors costing tens of thousands of dollars have been purchased for $500.

Of course, since all sales are final, use caution. Inspect the merchandise carefully before submitting a bid. If need be, hire an expert to inspect the property.

Lastly, using this medium of purchase takes time and effort if you are to maximize its profit potential. Sometimes the bidding is heavy, while other times you'll have little or no competition.

Regardless of its possible drawbacks, government surplus sales can be so lucrative that every individual, and certainly all businesses, should avail themselves of the opportunity.

THE EQUAL CREDIT OPPORTUNITY ACT

The Equal Credit Opportunity Act (ECOA) makes it illegal for any lender to discriminate against an applicant for credit based on race, color, religion, national origin, sex, marital status, or age. Further, it is unlawful to deny credit because all or part of the applicant's income is derived from public assistance, and/or because the applicant has, in good faith, exercised his or her rights under the Consumer Credit Protection Act.

While most laws pertaining to lending treat consumer and business credit differently, the ECOA doesn't, in a strict interpretive sense. The act is concerned with creditor's discrimination, not the actual extension of credit. So, whether you're looking for a car loan or money for your business, you have rights under this act. The act's purpose is to promote fair credit availability to creditworthy applicants. Its intent is to insure the evaluation of whether or not credit extended to an applicant is made on its merits and the applicants willingness and ability to repay the debt.

I don't like government intervention in what is supposed to be our free market. Clearly, based on history, government does more harm than good most of the time. However, I do support the ECOA, because lender abuses in this area are legendary. Continual abuses like red-lining had to be stopped. Congress, after giving financial institutions decades to change their ways, became convinced (at the strong urging of various civil rights and consumer groups) that, on their own, they would not do so. Hence, the passage of the ECOA and other consumer protection laws.

The act is broad in scope, but our outline will help you easily understand your rights. You may also benefit from advice from an attorney who specializes in financial discrimination. The following will help you determine if you should pursue a complaint.

The Act states it is NOT discriminatory for a lender to:

1. Ask you your marital status, as long as doing so is not used to discriminate in a determination of creditworthiness.

2. Ask your age and/or whether or not any or all of your income is derived from public assistance, as long as doing so is not used to discriminate in a determination of creditworthiness.

3. Use a scoring system that uses age as a factor in the determination of loan approval, as long as the age of the elderly is not assigned a negative value.

4. Ask the age of the applicant, as long as the age factor for his or her loan will then be used as a plus factor in the granting of credit.

If you're a woman applicant the lender CANNOT:

1. Discourage you from applying for credit based on your sex or marital status.

2. Deny you credit in your name only if you're creditworthy — even if you're married.

3. Inquire as to your birth-control practices or childbearing intentions.

4. Require a co-signer, if they would not do so for male applicants with the same application.

5. Change the conditions of your lending account solely because your marital status has changed.

6. Ask for, in your application for credit, information regarding your husband, unless he too will use the loan, you live in a community property state, you are relying on his income for loan approval, or you are applying for a student loan.

7. Even though it may be on the application, require that you use a title, such as Miss, Mrs., or Ms.

8. Deny you, even if you're married, the right to use your birth name as opposed to married name.

9. Refuse to accept as income any alimony or child support payments you receive, if you include them on your application. However, once you exercise that option, the lender has the right to require that you prove those payments and their reliability.

In general a lender CANNOT:

1. Refuse to take into consideration a wife's income in a joint application.

2. Refuse to take into account any additional information the applicant may offer regarding the past credit history of their previous spouse. This prevents a wife, for example, from being hounded by the unwillingness of her divorced husband to pay his bills during their marriage.

3. Report a joint accounts credit history in just the name of one party. This allows both spouses to receive the benefit of their credit rating. This, under normal circumstances, is important to housewives.

What can you gain by exercising your rights under the ECOA? Any lender who fails to meet their consumer credit obligations is liable for damages. These may include, but are not limited to, out-of-pocket losses, embarrassment, damage to credit reputation, and mental anguish. Punitive damages can also be applied. In an individual case, the applicant can recover up to $10,000.00. In a class action suit, the class can recover up to $500,000.00 or 1% of the net worth of the lender, whichever is less. Additionally, the ECOA provides relief for attorney fees and court costs for successful cases.

If you believe you've been discriminated against in any lending transaction, you should contact the following:

STATE BANKS:
> Office of Consumer Affairs
> F.D.I.C.
> 550 Seventeenth St., NW
> Washington, DC 20429
> (202) 898-3536

NATIONAL BANKS:
> Consumer Exams Division
> Comptroller of the Currency
> 490 L'Enfant Plaza, SW
> Washington, DC 20219
> (202) 447-1600

SAVINGS & LOAN:
> Office of Community Investment
> Federal Home Loan Bank Board
> 1700 G Street, NW, Fifth Floor
> Washington, DC 20552
> (202) 377-6237

CREDIT UNION:
> National Credit Union Administration
> 1776 G Street, NW
> Washington, DC 20456
> (202) 357-1065

OTHER CREDITORS:
> Office of Credit Practices
> Bureau of Consumer Protection
> Federal Trade Commission
> Washington, DC 20580
> (202) 724-1139

Financial discrimination is perhaps the worst discrimination of all as, in the real world, money, or access to money, is power. If you're denied that access, you have been denied a substantial portion of your financial rights, and that may completely change your life in a most negative sense. Unfortunately, this power of granting credit has been habitually abused. And not just by second rate players like finance companies. The truth is, some of the biggest offenders have been major money center banks. Again, I abhor government intervention. However, as financial institutions have a government-sanctioned, taxpayer-subsidized monopoly, their historical abuses cannot be tolerated. The results are too personally damaging. That's why we have the ECOA. That's why you must use this book. That's why you should understand it, and use it when necessary.

PRIVATE SOURCES OF EDUCATIONAL AID

In addition to the substantial number of governmental student aid programs there are numerous private sources that should be explored.

Where can they be located? Start with:

1. HIGH SCHOOL COUNSEL OFFICE.
2. LOCAL LIBRARY.
3. COLLEGE ADMINISTRATION OFFICE.
4. STATE SCHOLARSHIP OFFICE.
5. Your state's DEPARTMENT OF EDUCATION.

What should you look for?

1. AWARDS AND/OR PRIZES.
2. MONETARY ASSISTANCE.
3. AID GRANTS.
4. ENDOWMENTS.
5. RESEARCH GRANTS.

When locating programs, ask for any directories, books, guides, newspapers, or newsletters that pertain to the subject or your area of study. Too many applicants are not successful, not for lack of educational assistance funds, but rather for the inability to find the programs for which they may qualify. That's why tens of millions of dollars of aid go unclaimed every year. That's not a misprint —tens of millions of dollars available to college students receive no applications.

The following is a listing of associations you may wish to contact. While limited, it shows the diversity of assistance available.

1. ETHNIC
Sons of Italy in America

219 E. Street, NE
Washington, DC
(202) 547-2900

2. EDUCATIONAL

The National Student Teaching Competition
NEA Student Program
1201 16th St., NW
Washington, DC 20036-3290

3. TRADE

International Association of Fire Chiefs
1329 18th St., NW
Washington, DC 20036

4. HONOR

The Honor Society of Phi Kappa Phi
P.O.Box 1600
Louisiana State University
Baton Rouge, LA 70893

5. RELIGIOUS

Association for Lutherans
Appleton, WI 54919

6. UNION

Communications Workers of America
1925 K St., NW
Washington, DC 20006

These are a few of the thousands of organizations that have money available to help you or your children receive a college education.

To locate others you should read one or all of the following. They can be purchased at most bookstores or located at your library.

1. THE COLLEGE COST PLANNER. To order, write P.O. Box 18623, Washington, DC 20077-2617. This is a monthly newsletter that lists college aid, grant sources, colleges with reasonable costs, and general guides.

2. NEED A LIFT. This annual brochure can be ordered by writing The American Legion, P.O. Box 1050, Indianapolis, IN 46206. It contains sources for educational benefits, private lending, grants, etc.

3. DIRECTORY OF RESEARCH GRANTS. Published by Onyx Press. It includes indexes for organizations, grants, etc.

4. FOUNDATION GRANTS TO INDIVIDUALS. A complete listing of foundations that have monies available. The directory is indexed by source, with addresses, tips, etc. To order directly: Foundation Center, 79 Fifth Avenue, New York, NY 10003.

5. FINANCIAL AID FOR HIGHER EDUCATION. Lists over 5,000 financial aid programs. Published yearly by William Brown Publishers.

6. ANNUAL REGISTER OF GRANT SUPPORT. Available from Marquis, 200 East Ohio St., Chicago, IL 60611. Lists over 2,000 grants programs.

7. THE COLLEGE COST BOOK. From College Board Publications, Box 886, New York, NY 10101. Listing for over 4,000 aid programs.

Here are some important tips when making application:

1. GET STARTED — NOW. Too many applicants start looking for aid a month or two before they're supposed to start school. Then, of course, it's too late. Because there are many, many sources, a search takes time. The sooner you start, the better your chances.

2. MAKE SURE YOUR SOURCES ARE CURRENT. If you use outdated sources, those more than a year old, you may be wasting valuable time by, for example, applying for a grant that is no longer available. Find the sources you

think applicable and contact them directly for their forms, outlines, etc.

3. DOUBLE CHECK YOUR APPLICATION. This sounds so simple, but it needs to be mentioned, as many applicants don't understand that you must fill out every line, even if the answer is, "NONE." If you skip questions, forget to sign the application, or write illegibly, your application will be returned and you will have lost many weeks or months.

4. BEAT THE DEADLINE. Aid programs have a deadline for application, as their budgets are yearly based. Miss by one day and you'll be rejected.

There are, as mentioned previously, many sources of governmental financial aid. However, few are aware of the many private programs. And that gives you a leg-up when making application. You may be, and this is not a rare occurrence, the only qualified applicant for an obscure program. And that means approval. The best aspect is, many private organizations give outright aid, as opposed to loan, which means you have no future financial obligation. This aid may be more than adequate to finance your children's educational requirements.

The money is there. All you have to do is expend a little effort locating those programs where you qualify. In terms of your higher education, there probably isn't a more important use of your time.

LOWER YOUR LOAN RATE

Most borrowers don't understand loan rates are nego-tiable. Each year, consumers pay millions more in interest than they should because they are unaware of this impor-tant fact. Unfortunately, in most lending transactions, the borrower is at a disadvantage due to the imbalance in the lender/borrower relationship; i.e., acquiring the loan is usu-ally more important to the individual than the cost of losing that individual's business is to the lender — which explains the arrogance of many lenders and the timidity of their cus-tomers.

As a rule, financial institutions have one interest rate per type of loan. They charge X percent for prime; X plus percent for home mortgages; X plus, plus percent for car loans; and so on. The reason for lumping loan rates by cate-gory, as opposed to relying on the individual's creditworthi-ness, is that the lender wants good loan customers to pay for the mistakes they make with others.

Let's review two borrowers buying the same make and model of car having the same price tag. One has been a bank customer for 10 years, has 60% down, needs the loan for only 24 months, and has a perfect credit rating. The other cus-tomer has been with the bank 6 months, has 10% down, needs the loan for 48 months, and has marginal credit. What loan rate will these customers be quoted? Regardless of the actual rate, it will be the same in each case. The effect of this sameness, as previously noted, is that the good customer pays a higher rate than his financial particulars would dic-tate, to cover the bank's loss in case the marginal customer defaults. That's the way most financial institutions do busi-ness — a direct contradiction to the premise that loan inter-est rates reflect the lender's exposure to risk on each indi-vidual request. If we are to take the bankers at their word that they function in a competitive market, these customers should have differing interest rates — substantially differ-ent rates.

Good financial institutions, those staffed by fair and knowledgeable loan officers, balance their loan portfolio on a risk basis. Institutions you shouldn't patronize — which unfortunately represent the majority — are those unresponsive to the needs of their community who lump their loan rates by category.

How can you combat this abuse? You have to shop your loans. A loan request should be shopped at a minimum of three institutions. That's the least you should do. Ideally you'll explore other non-traditional avenues, such as private lending, etc. You should also remember this valuable rule of thumb: bank at the smallest, or one of the smaller, F.D.I.C. insured financial institutions in your market. The smaller bank needs you and gives your loan leverage, a big bank doesn't. For example, a $10,000.00 car loan at a $10 million dollar bank is equal to a $10 million dollar loan at a $10 billion dollar bank. That leveraged positioning facilitates loan rate negotiations. Most large lenders have a we-do-it-our-way-or-else attitude. That's going to cost you added loan interest.

You have to convince your bank, without being abusive, that you know how the system works and are not willing to pay extra interest because they have delinquent loan problems. Further, you see yourself as the banks best possible loan risk, meaning, based on your credit history and banking relationship, you aren't a risk at all. Consequently, you expect to be in the bank's lowest loan rate category.

Use whatever dialogue fits your style. This positioning is quite easy once you get the hang of it. Many of my consulting clients, following my recommendation, have reported they received a rate reduction by simply taking the initiative and asking. Be advised, however, in larger institutions this may not work because they don't think they need your business. But, if that's their attitude, I suggest you immediately move your accounts to a bank that will appreciate them.

How important is this subject? The following helps crystallize the point: a minuscule reduction of one-quarter of one percentage point on the average $100,000 thirty-year mortgage saves almost $6,800 in repayment costs. A one-half percentage point reduction approximates savings of $13,500. A one percentage point reduction, a goal you should be able to meet or exceed, saves close to $27,000. That's why you have to negotiate your loan rates — there's too much at stake. And that's true whether it's a small business, mortgage, car, or personal loan.

LENDING? GET A CONTRACT

Many lending transactions are not of the traditional bank/consumer variety — they are between friends or relatives. Normally there is no paperwork associated with this exchange of money. The reason for this mistake is a misplaced trust and/or lack of understanding of the laws that pertain to the owing of money.

Borrowing that involves relatives is usually left to the goodwill of the parties, as no one wants the other to feel they aren't trusted. Then too, it's all in the family.

The same emotions are present when lending to friends. If you know someone well enough to lend them money, you may be reluctant to ask for documentation. Conversely, if you are asking to borrow money, you may feel hurt that your friend or family member doesn't trust you — after all, isn't that what signing a note implies?

In these transactions, assuming a contract was requested, comments are made to the effect, "If I wanted to be treated like this I could have gone to a bank." Of course, that's more bravado than fact, but that's not the point.

The problem with not documenting lending agreements is there are often misunderstandings. People hear what they want to hear. They remember what they want to remember. The lender recollects one thing, the borrower another. The courts are jammed with cases like this, and they all could have been avoided. Obviously, regardless which side of the transaction you're on, getting it in writing makes sense.

The above, while important, probably isn't enough to convince some of you. Fortunately, for those who doubt, there are other considerations to make the point. What happens if one of the parties is killed or dies? The lender may have to turn to the estate to be repaid. However, without documentation the executor or court isn't likely to honor the debt. This unforeseen circumstance defines a lending contract as mandatory. Make up your own scenario — no matter what the circumstances, the advantage of having it in writing makes sense.

Clearly, not having it in writing can cause more problems than asking for a signature could ever raise. As embarrassing as doing things correctly can sometimes be, it's not as bad as ending up in court suing a relative or friend. Or, it's not as bad as suing their estate and perhaps having their surviving relatives think you are trying to cheat them out of a part of their inheritance.

The worst part of this error in judgement; i.e., lending on faith alone, is getting it in writing is not that complicated. Once having explained the requirement to the borrower, you don't need an attorney to make the matter legal. A handwritten signed note that outlines the understanding of both parties is more than enough. That said, I recommend going to your local stationery store and purchasing a fill-in-the-blank note/contract of the variety you require. Most stores have a complete compliment of installment, single payment, secured, unsecured, balloon, and mortgage notes. Complete it, sign it, make a copy for the borrower, and retain the original. These notes usually cost less than a dollar. I might also mention that many publishing companies offer legal form books or kits for $50 or less. They include fill-in-the-blank forms for almost any transaction you can think of, including lending. Perhaps, depending on your needs, you will wish to invest in one for your financial library.

Remember, when someone asks to borrow money, it is completely appropriate for you to ask for something far less expensive in return: their signature. Doing so doesn't mean you don't trust them. Quite the contrary. It's simply an acknowledgement that circumstances can occur which may supersede both parties good intentions. It protects the lender, it protects the borrower.

As anyone who has had difficulty collecting an undocumented loan can attest, failure to follow my advice can cost you more than the money involved.

COSIGNING A LOAN

At some point in your life you may be asked to cosign a loan. Before you commit your finances, you should know that as many as three out of four cosigners are subsequently asked to pay the debt. That's a rather startling statistic, especially in light of the fact that a cosigner receives none of the loan proceeds.

That alone should ensure you never cosign a loan for anyone, but in those rare instances where you feel obligated, you should understand the following:

1. Make sure you can afford to pay the debt in its entirety. Again, the odds say you will have to. If you cannot afford the expense, remember this: your credit rating can be destroyed by non-payment, attachments can be made that may jeopardize you assets and net worth, and your wages may be garnished.

2. When you cosign a loan you may be lowering your ability to acquire financing needed for other purposes. On your personal loan application, you have to indicate cosigning as a contingent liability, which most lenders deem a first-line obligation. Hence, that cosigned loan may mean your personal loan is denied, as the lender will not extend additional credit.

3. Upon default, your total obligation may be far in excess of the loan's principal. For instance, you may be assessed legal fees, court costs, collection expenses, and/or additional interest.

4. You may be asked to pay the note in full immediately if the borrower is delinquent even a few days. The lender, in most cases, is under no obligation to make extended efforts to collect from the person who received the loan proceeds. In fact, in

some instances they make very little effort to collect from them. They will go to the cosigner because it's easier, faster, less hassle, and they stand a much better chance of collecting.

5. The lender is not necessarily obligated to give you copies of the loan documentation, so you may not completely understand your commitment and all its ramifications.

6. If you pledged an asset for collateral, it could be lost in case of default.

Here are a few steps you can take that will help your position if you decide to cosign a loan:

1. Never pledge a specific asset when cosigning, especially one that is easily repossessed.

2. Have the lender include a statement in the loan documentation that you are responsible for the loan principal and nothing else. In many cases the lender will agree when asked. If they won't, the loan is probably so bad you should rethink your decision.

3. Have the lender include a statement indicating they are required to notify you immediately if the borrower defaults by even one day. That way you can start making calls and taking actions that need to be made to protect your position. If you're notified immediately you can, if necessary, make the monthly payment before the grace period expires, which will keep the loan up-to-date. In that way it won't be called and the entire balance demanded, and you'll save the late payment charge.

4. Ensure that you get copies of all loan documentation. Make sure you understand it. Remember, the odds say you will be asked to pay this loan, so it's best to know the extent of your obligation.

5. In many states, a cosigner has additional rights over and above those allowed by federal law — review them prior to signing the guarantee.

I strongly recommend you don't cosign a loan. But if you do, you may wish to get a free copy of *The Credit Practices Rule* and *Solving Credit Problems*. Write: Public Reference, Federal Trade Commission (FTC), Washington, DC 20580.

One final note: 75% of all cosigners are asked to pay the cosigned debt. I reiterate that point, as nothing puts a cosigner's position in more perspective. The facts speak for themselves. Borrowers who need a cosigner default far more often than they pay. That's why they need a cosigner. If, for whatever reason, you decide to buck the odds, don't be disappointed or angered when you have to start making payments or pay the loan in full.

SOLVING A PROBLEM WITH YOUR BANK

Most of us have had a problem with our bank at one time or another. Some are simple, some are not. If your bank is typical, solving the dispute will be more than difficult, no matter what the circumstances. For some reason, banks feel they are above the normal concerns of a service business. Consequently, they are not as consumer responsive as one would expect. To the contrary, as opposed to solving matters, they oftentimes make things much worse.

The surest test of a bank's ability to meet the grandiose claims of its advertisements is how it reacts when there is a difficulty or dispute. Any bank can be friendly when things are going smoothly, but few meet their service claims when a customer has a problem.

Of course, the best way to avoid a problem with your bank is to do preventive maintenance prior to one occurring. To that end, you should bank at the smallest, or one of the smaller institutions in your market area. The small bank wants to become a big bank and the way they accomplish that is to have a large number of satisfied customers. Many big banks erroneously believe they don't need the average customer, and their attitude reflects that thinking. In short, they don't care if you're unhappy or have a problem.

Next, after establishing your account, it's wise to introduce yourself to as many of the bank officers and staff as possible. Make sure you meet the President, Cashier, and Chief Loan Officer. These three will be able to solve most, if not all, your bank problems. The head of bookkeeping and Head Teller are two more who shouldn't be overlooked, as they are the frontline people who may solve a problem before you are forced to seek a bank officer.

If you do have a problem, direct it to the proper chain-of-command. This alone can save you wasted time and effort. One of the reasons customers get shuffled around is they start out in the wrong department when they first ask for assistance.

The following will help the bank help you:

1. TELLER — HEAD TELLER — CASHIER —
VICE PRESIDENT OPERATIONS —EXECUTIVE
VICE PRESIDENT —PRESIDENT — BOARD OF
DIRECTORS.

2. LOAN CLERK — LOAN OFFICER — VICE
PRESIDENT LOANS — EXECUTIVE VICE
PRESIDENT — PRESIDENT — BOARD OF DI-
RECTORS.

3. BOOKKEEPER — DEPARTMENT HEAD —
CASHIER — VICE PRESIDENT OPERATIONS —
EXECUTIVE VICE PRESIDENT —PRESI-
DENT — BOARD OF DIRECTORS.

These are the basic chains-of-command you'll need. The
individual titles may vary, but not enough to confuse.

Here are a few examples to show how this works. If you
have a problem with a check being returned against your account, where should you turn? Start with the department
that issued the notice, which in this case would be bookkeeping. Begin with a bookkeeper and work your way up until receiving satisfaction. Don't give up, as a tactful yet aggressive
bank consumer can almost always get his or her way. The
bottomline is, be assertive to the point where you will settle
for nothing less than a fair resolution. After all, that's what
the bank is supposed to do in the first place. Another example: you can't cash a third party check. Start with the chain
that begins with a teller.

If you control the situation, start in the proper chain-of-
command, politely demand results, and are willing to go to
the Board of Directors if necessary, you'll normally be rewarded with positive results. But what happens when that
doesn't work? It depends on the severity of the difficulty.
You have at your disposal a number of banking agencies
that may be of help. However, it must be noted that contact-

ing a bank regulatory agency can be a frustrating experience. In too many instances the regulators are more concerned with protecting the bank than solving your problem. However, as banks don't like to answer letters from Washington, they may, once they realize that you're serious, decide to help rather than be bothered further.

If that doesn't work, you always have legal recourse. I am ignoring a major legal battle, which would obviously require representation from an attorney who specializes in financial litigations. For other, less complicated cases, small claims court is the battlefield of choice. For example, if you've been assessed an overdraft fee in error and the bank won't return the charge, once the bank is served with papers, they may decide it's better to comply with your request than spend perhaps ten times the OD charge to argue. Then too, most banks don't want the potential embarrassment of having a number of bank officers trying publicly to explain a depositor's complaint in front of a jury. For information regarding small claims in your state, ask the court clerk for their brochure.

Remember, start inside the bank, and make every effort to resolve matters with the least possible aggravation. Talk to the proper department, and go all the way to the top if you don't receive satisfaction. When those channels are closed, ask for regulatory assistance and/or head for small claims court.

Unfortunately, bank/banker arrogance has bullied the public into believing: (1) Banks don't make errors, (2) whatever the problem, it's your fault, (3) you have to pay for the error regardless of who's responsible, and (4) the bank can't be beaten in an adversarial proceeding. All four are misconceptions.

OBTAINING FEDERAL RECORDS

When discussing how to obtain federal records under the Freedom of Information Act (FOIA) the question that should occur to most is, what does the subject have to do with finances?

Let's review just a few possible answers.

1. YOU CAN LEARN IF THE F.B.I. HAS A FILE ON YOU. An important fact if you have made an application for government assistance lending.

2. YOU CAN OBTAIN REPORTS FROM THE CONSUMER PRODUCTS SAFETY COMMISSION REGARDING PRODUCTS THAT MAY POSE A SAFETY HAZARD. If you have experienced a problem, or were injured by the product, that report may make your case in court.

3. YOU CAN RECEIVE COPIES OF INSPECTION REPORTS ON NURSING HOMES CERTIFIED FOR MEDICARE. That information has both financial and personal applications.

5. YOU CAN OBTAIN INFORMATION FROM THE DEPARTMENT OF LABOR REGARDING PLANT SAFETY AT YOUR PLACE OF EMPLOYMENT. Here too, there are personal and financial considerations, especially if you've recently been injured at work and need to file a possibly disputed claim.

6. FOIA APPLIES TO EXTREMELY COMPLICATED AND COSTLY FINANCIAL RESEARCH ABOUT SUCH THINGS AS THE STOCK MARKET, THE BANKING INDUSTRY, THE MONEY SUPPLY, ETC. This information has unlimited financial ramifications in both the private and business sector of our economy. The fact is, businesses are paying large sums of research money to ascertain much of the same information the government will give you for free.

These are just a few examples of the correlation between obtaining government documentation and finances. Due to the nature of the subject and the scope of the government's interests, the list could go on indefinitely. If you've thought of it, chances are the government has a report on it.

As you might expect, there are limitations to what one can receive. In some cases the exemptions make sense, in others they don't. In those cases where you think you've been unfairly denied information, you may appeal. We'll get to that shortly.

The FOIA gives government agencies the right to refuse information under the following exemption guidelines:

1. CLASSIFIED AND NATIONAL DEFENSE SECRETS.

2. INFORMATION PROHIBITED BY ANOTHER LAW.

3. INFORMATION THAT WOULD BE PROHIBITED UNDER THE PERSONAL PRIVACY ACT (as it pertains to another).

4. INFORMATION BY AGENCIES THAT HAVE RESPONSIBILITY FOR NATIONAL AND F.D.I.C. INSURED BANKS.

5. CERTAIN MATERIALS FROM LAW ENFORCEMENT AGENCIES.

6. SOME INTER AND INTRA AGENCY MEMOS AND OTHER COMMUNICATIONS.

7. CONFIDENTIAL AGENCY RULES AND REGULATIONS.

These are just a few of the exemptions. Now, before you get discouraged, remember this. The application of these exemptions is totally subjective, and administered by the agency FOIA Officer. In many cases, people are amazed at what information they have received with a specific request. These guidelines of exemptions were designed to cover any and all situations, if needed. They are not always applied. Even at that, don't forget we can appeal a denial.

Also, it should be noted that the FOIA does not apply to Congress, the court system, and state and local governments. However, many states have enacted their own FOIA, so to find out what's available where you live, contact your state's Attorney General. The information obtained locally may be even more valuable than what can be obtained in Washington.

There is no central FOIA office. All applications for information must be sent to the agency's FOIA Officer. For example, if you want information from the Department of Labor, you have to write them directly.

A word of caution. While this noncentralization makes sense from the government's point of view, it can inhibit your search. Often times the information is available, but the application goes to the wrong agency. That's why you have to apply to any agency that might have what you are looking for. Look in your phone book and find the number of your nearest Federal Information Center, they'll help direct your inquiries. Or if you want more specific information, write the Government Printing Office, Washington, D.C. 20402 and ask for a copy of the *Consumers Resource Handbook*, the *US Government Handbook*, and *Your Right to Federal Records*. The first two books describe government agencies and what they supervise and administer. That will give you direction for your applications. The last booklet will give you a detailed review of the FOIA.

1. GETTING STARTED. Obtaining FOIA information is as easy as writing a letter. However, you must try and give the FOIA Officer as much information as possible to assist him in meeting your needs. Don't think you can go on a fishing expedition, because you can't. The FOIA Officer is only required to make a reasonable effort to be of assistance, so detailing your request only makes sense.

Here is a sample letter to show you how easy this really is:

Date
FOIA OFFICER
Name of Agency
Address

Dear FOIA Officer:

Under the Freedom of Information Act, 5 U.S.C. 552, I am requesting access to, or copies of _____ (identify the material as much as possible).

If you deny any or all of this request, please site the specific exemption you think justifies your refusal and notify me of my appeal procedures available under the present law.

If there are any fees for copying and/or searching records, please let me know before you complete my request (this is optional).

If you have any questions regarding this matter, you may call me direct at 312-555-5555 (home), or at 312-555-5556 (business). (This too is optional.)

Yours very truly,

Name
Address

That's all there is to it. You have met the requirements for an FOIA application.

In the letter you have one additional option available. Research indicates that if you give the reason for your request, you may have more luck than if you ask for same cold. I assume this is nothing more than a result of human nature, but it does seem to work. If you decide to use this technique, it should be inserted right after the first paragraph. The more harmless you make your reasoning, the more success you will have.

2. FEES. If the agency is able to assist you, they have the right to charge $4 to $26 per hour in search fees. However, in all my requests (and I've had my share), I have never been charged one dollar. It's a fee they can charge, not one they automatically charge. You do have to be careful, which is why I inserted the paragraph in our request that will allow us to make a cost decision before running up a bill.

Also, they can charge $.25 or less per copy. Again, I have never been charged anything, but you can't rely on that.

One final thought on costs. If you can convince the agency that the information will benefit the general public, the fees are negotiable, or they may be waived entirely, regardless of how big they would have been. Possibly another reason for including your request reasoning in your application.

Don't forget, FOIA Officers can be as subjective as the next guy, so it pays to play-the-game and tell them what they want to hear. Playing tough with any government agency or representative will almost always get you nothing, except trouble.

3. TIME LIMITS. The agency has ten days from the time of receipt to answer your request. If it can't meet that deadline, and needs additional research time through their agency or others, it must inform you prior to the ten day limit.

My experience shows that most requests will not be completed during that time. This is another of those governmental show-but-no-go regulations in that it looks good, but there is no enforcement procedure, and/or penalty if they don't comply.

Regardless, if your ten days is up, and you can't wait another couple of weeks, write another letter reminding the FOIA Officer of your request. Don't do this unless absolutely necessary, as when you do, you severely cut your chances of receiving what you want. However, there may be cases where it will be necessary, but use caution and tact.

4. WHAT TO DO IF YOU'RE REFUSED. As mentioned earlier, you have the right to appeal an exemption denial. You can even go so far as to file a FOIA lawsuit in Federal District Court. But this is extreme, as the costs would be prohibitive, even though you may win court and attorney's fees if the case is found in your favor.

I won't go into the specifics of an appeal, because there are many, depending on the reasoning of the denial. That's why I included the paragraph about appeal procedures in the request letter. They'll supply what you need.

Again, referring to experience, appeals don't get much done. To really have weight, you would have to resort to a court remedy and, in most cases, the expense would not be cost-justified. Maybe it is for a major newspaper trying for a scoop, but for the average person, no.

However, you probably won't be turned down, so don't worry about it. The reason I bring up the subject of federal records is to make you aware of inexhaustible financial records that may offer you a profit, and that information is seldom denied.

5. THE BOTTOMLINE. Federal records are available for those who know how to use the system. It is my sincere belief that some of those records can make or save you money. This applies to personal and business finances.

All it takes is a short letter and the cost of a stamp. In return you can have copies of government financial studies that cost perhaps hundreds of thousands of dollars. The information contained may well be worth a small fortune in the right hands.

AVOIDING SWINDLES

There are more people being swindled today than ever before. You'd think, with all the consumerism of the last decade, that the numbers would be going down, not up, but that's not the case.

There are many ways you can lose your hard-earned money. Most swindles involve shoddy merchandise, excessive interest costs, paying too much for merchandise at the time of purchase, or poor service once the purchase has been made. Outright fraud, while certainly a substantial percentage of swindles, is not, as you might imagine, the main cause of people being ripped-off. Successful swindles usually involve part real deal and part quasi-fraud. That's why they are hard to avoid, they are not terribly obvious.

Most people are aware of major league cons, like the pigeon drop, and therefore can avoid being a victim. But that's not where the real threat exists. If you are swindled, it's probably going to be a deal that sounds, on its face, semi-reasonable. One that, if it was offered by a reputable company, would be a bargain.

That means you have to be discerning and do your homework before spending a dollar in any one of the following possible frauds:

1. GET RICH QUICK SCHEMES. To many this may seem obvious, but the fact is, this is the easiest con to sell. It almost always appeals to someone because of the greed factor. Others, unfortunately, are desperate and want to believe that their financial lives can be changed quickly and painlessly.

These opportunity ads offer easy answers to difficult problems. Some involve offers for jobs, businesses, or riches without describing the actual plan or product.

2. INVESTMENTS BY PHONE. If you've got a phone, you're on a con artist's list somewhere, so be alert. These guys are good.

It should be easy not to be conned like this but, here too, this is one of the most successful swindles. The answer is, don't invest money with anyone who calls you out of the blue. Legitimate investment firms don't do business this way.

Sometimes they offer tax shelters, gold-in-the-ground schemes, or securities. It doesn't matter what or how good the deal sounds, you're better off hanging up.

3. WORK AT HOME OFFERS. Many have started their own business at home, which can be a viable and profitable alternative to the traditional work environment. That's why this swindle hooks people. Everyone knows someone success-ful who works at home. Therefore the concept sounds rea-sonable.

Unfortunately, although there probably are exceptions, what these programs are selling is their product, not a legit-imate home business. Some schemes are down to earth, like typing manuscripts. Others are more exotic, like raising chinchillas. The most common is addressing envelopes. Re-gardless of the come-on, they all involve purchasing some-thing from the advertiser. You get stuck with his merchan-dise, only to find out there is no market for whatever you're producing.

If you've got an idea for a home business, fine. If some-one else has one you can buy into, forget it.

4. LAND DEALS. Once very popular, this swindle died out about fifteen years ago after extensive publicity. But, like all things, the cycle has come full circle and the land con is back. People have forgotten and/or a whole new genera-tion of potential victims are now adults.

Don't buy land sight unseen. It's that simple. Forget the brochures. Go look at it. If you're interested after inspecting your potential purchase, review the contract carefully, very carefully. Virtually everyone who buys land being sold in this manner is disappointed and subsequently loses money when they resell the property at nickels on the dollar.

5. INTEREST RATE CONS. Some swindles don't happen with the merchandise purchase. They occur with the interest on the retail installment contract.

The merchandise may be excellent, but it's always sold via credit. Granted you can pay cash, but the thrust of the advertising is to encourage monthly installments. Too many fall for the credit offer without ever putting a pencil to the bottomline. The interest rate on the contract is unbelievably high, so what was a good deal from a purchase price standpoint becomes a rip-off in total cost.

Many catalog companies work this way, even some that are generally accepted as reputable.

6. VANITY SALES. If a product is being sold that promises to make you taller, grow hair, make you younger looking, develop your bust, or reduce your weight by some strange sounding means, you are about to waste money.

Vanity cons are a big, big business. The reasoning is simple enough, as we all would like things to be better than they are. However, that doesn't happen by taking a pill or rubbing on a cream.

These swindles are usually sold through a cheap magazine or a direct mail piece. They're easy to spot.

7. HOME REPAIRS. Don't deal with a home repair contractor you didn't call. Good ones don't sell their services door-to-door, and yet every year, especially in winter and spring, they come out of the woodwork to prey on the elderly and those living in neighborhoods in need of repair.

What starts out to be a small repair ends up being a major expense and then isn't finished correctly and/or the contractor disappears.

I'm all for saving money, but if you try to have your home repaired on the cheap, you usually double your actual cost.

Check out your contractor.

8. YOU'VE WON A PRIZE. This is a new scam born during the last couple of years. Hardly a day goes by that you don't "win a prize" in some contest you can't remember or a drawing that came from a mailing list.

These are perhaps the easiest cons to avoid, because they all require you to spend money in some manner, either for merchandise that you get at a discount, which is supposedly your prize, or for shipping and handling.

Legitimate companies don't ask their prize winners to spend a dime to collect their prize.

9. GHOULS. Swindlers have no class. This shows how low they will go with their con. It works like this: They read the obituaries and send the surviving spouse a bill or unordered merchandise in the name of the deceased.

This works, almost without fail, because of the confusion during this time of grief and stress, and the fact that everyone wants to honor the commitments of their spouse. Widows are a special favorite target of obituary cons.

If you get a bill or merchandise under these circumstances and you're not absolutely sure of the transaction, don't pay until you are.

10. INHERITANCE BROKERS. While there are some in the field of finance who actually track down money that belongs to heirs, most of these arrangements are unsatisfactory.

This is a multi-million dollar industry. Sadly, the millions aren't collected by the rightful owners of lost inheritances, but rather in fees paid to the brokers by the public. Actual recoveries are rare and usually small.

The key in telling a con from a legitimate operator is that reputable firms charge a percentage of the found money for their service. The swindler wants an up-front fee in addition to a percentage.

11. BAIT & SWITCH. You'd think everyone would know to avoid this sample con, but, as it is still practiced in many stores, apparently that's not the case.

If you see merchandise advertised and then the salesman talks you out of purchasing that product, only to replace it with another, more costly version of what you need, leave the store immediately.

Even if you would be happy with the higher priced merchandise, since you now know how these people do business, think of how you will be treated if you have a problem later.

12. CURES THROUGH THE MAIL. Here too, like the obituary ghouls, swindlers hit bottom. They are not above selling worthless cures for deadly diseases, knowing that those afflicted are desperate.

This is not only a scam, it's a deadly scam, as many ill people turn their back on traditional methods in favor of pills they purchased from companies that advertise in supermarket tabloids.

All methods of treatment should be explored for every illness, but whatever you decide is best for you should be offered by people you know and trust. Don't let desperation or fear make you a target for additional grief and danger.

13. CONTESTS. If you like contests that's fine. However, don't enter ones offered through the mail that require you to send money. Contests that have a step-by-step approach are the most costly; i.e., the first five, six, seven, or whatever number of contests are easy so you always qualify for the next step on the way to the Grand Prize. Of course, you have to send in $X with every entry. Then the final step is very difficult, if not impossible. Even if you do win, you will have to share your prize with others, which means you receive but a fraction of the advertised award. This scam starts out very innocently, costing only a few dollars. Once you're hooked you don't want to let go because you have time and money invested and you believe you're so close to winning.

The best bet is not to get started in the first place.

14. REPOSSESSED MERCHANDISE. Repossessed or unclaimed merchandise may be a good deal. It may also be a gigantic rip-off.

The con is, the merchandise was never repossessed or unclaimed. It's just their way of selling by appealing to the greed of the buyer. Instead of receiving quality merchandise at a fraction of its cost, what you end up with is shoddy overpriced merchandise.

The way to avoid being taken is to know the company. If you don't, or if the firm always has repossessed or unclaimed property, it's best to shop elsewhere. Knowing the company's reputation also holds true when shopping at going-out-of-business sales. Although it's against the law in most instances, many retailers go out of business yearly. Even if they're caught, the fine is minimal, which is why it pays to ignore the legalities.

15. THE CAR CON. When you're buying a car, new or used, you have to understand the dealer has many ways to separate you from your money. You have to use caution.

One con is to offer a great trade-in on your car, more than you know it's worth. The sting is, the new car is so grossly overinflated that the dealership can afford to overpay your trade and still make a huge profit.

Car cons are too numerous to detail. The best advice I can offer is, buy a consumer guide so you know what your car and the new car are worth before you go to the dealership. Don't allow yourself to be "worked" by the sale's staff. Know what you are willing to pay. When the deal exceeds that, walk. There are plenty of dealers.

16. DOOR TO DOOR SYMPATHY SALES. Door to door sales crews are often taught to sell through sympathy. They will use a front such as a charity to sell you magazines or whatever. Few are actually connected to a charity. They are there to sell and will do whatever necessary to accomplish that goal — even lie.

If you don't know the individual, it's best to stay away from door-to-door sales. While some may be legitimate, most are not. Don't take chances. Odds are that you will not be helping the charity and you'll never see your magazine.

Obviously, I cannot possibly cover all swindles. I offer the examples above to explain the most widely used and to give a feel for the workings of a con. They all work, to varying degrees, on the greed or sympathy of the victim. Here are some simple warning signs:

1. SOMETHING FOR NOTHING.

2. CONTRACT WORDING YOU DON'T UNDERSTAND.

3. CONSTANT PRESSURE TO COMPLETE THE DEAL QUICKLY.

4. A SALESMAN YOU DON'T FEEL COMFORTABLE WITH.

5. A SALESMAN YOU FEEL TOO COMFORTABLE WITH.

6. AN ESCALATING DEAL. YOU HAVE TO SPEND MORE MONEY AT EVERY TURN.

7. A COMPANY YOU DON'T KNOW.

8. SOLICITATION AT HOME.

Be skeptical. Pay by check. Know your dealer. Don't sign anything you don't thoroughly understand. And never buy without shopping around.

There are more than one thousand different swindles presently being practiced. You have to protect yourself. As my consulting experience has proven, under the right circumstances, anyone can be a victim.

TELEMARKETING FRAUD

Let's start with some significant facts:

1. ALMOST 75% OF ALL FINANCIAL FRAUD
COMPLAINTS INVESTIGATED BY GOVERN-
MENT AGENCIES INVOLVE TELEMARKETNG.

2. TELEMARKETING FRAUD COSTS CONSUMERS
OVER ONE BILLION DOLLARS A YEAR.

3. VIRTUALLY NONE OF THE AVERAGE $5,000.00
PER VICTIM LOSS IS EVER RECOVERED.

Telemarketing is a legitimate selling method, so I caution not to paint all telemarketers with the same brush.
Notwithstanding that admonishment, research indicates the
risk of doing business over the phone adds substantial exposure to the already risky investment arena.

Typically, the consumer receives a call out of the blue
from an individual or company he doesn't know. Within seconds the caller is pitching one of a wide variety of exotic financial potpourri, such as oil leases, tax shelters, gold-in-
the-ground schemes, etc. Part of the scam includes statements like, "You are on our recommended list of investors . . . timing is the key, and the time is now . . . this investment has no risk and the profits are unlimited." There is
always urgency for you to make a decision. Pressure is part
of their strategy. Of course, the main ingredient of their success is the personal greed of those they call. In interviews, I
am constantly struck by the fact that almost all those who
have fallen victim to a phone hustler would, after the fact,
admit they should have known better. "All the warning signs
were there, but, those returns, and the man said I couldn't
lose."

Even those who show some caution are quite often
taken. They ask for references, brochures, and the like, and

in some cases that thankfully ends the conversation. But, the more sophisticated cons have a brochure as well as reference shills who will gladly tell prospective investors they made a million. The point is, a high class telemarketing fraud may not be able to be detected by taking normal precautions.

Remembering that the average loss is $5,000.00, you have to wonder what the victim was thinking about. If someone walked up to you on the street and asked for that sum, would you give it to them? Of course not. Yet, because they have a good phone pitch and know how to play on one's greed, that's exactly what millions of Americans do every year. They promise so much that common sense becomes tranquilized. Years of financial education is put in moth balls because a fast talker vows results no investment can possibly produce.

Another important point: if the caller could do what they promised, they wouldn't be talking to you. They wouldn't waste time trying to make you a dollar. They would be investing their own funds, or every dollar they could borrow, and reaping the benefits. Simply put, when's the last time anyone, even a friend, did you a financial favor that made you a big return? Never? Me too, and that makes clear that strangers over the phone probably won't either.

I have to state, for perspective, contrary to what you might think, most victims of financial telemarketing fraud are not little old ladies (please excuse any negative connotation of that term, it's used as reference only), but doctors, lawyers, bankers, and investors with years of experience. The reason? My educated guess is that greed knows no social or financial status boundaries. Others, the less affluent, the elderly, get involved in these schemes because they don't understand, are scared, or allow themselves to become pressured, thereby leading to a poor decision. A revealing feature of the problem is that people who should know better make up the largest segment of the casualty list.

A top-quality telemarketing financial scam is not, as previously noted, easily discernible. Yet, if you understand the concept, even the best show red flags. Phrases like, " . . . can't miss . . . the opportunity of a lifetime . . . double your money . . . we need your check in 48 hours . . . ," mean you probably have a problem. Watch for warning statements, as, since not all cons are alike, things can become confusing. Telemarketing frauds sell anything and everything so you can't rely on a list of investments to beware of. You may be minutes into the conversation before you realize that a pitch is underway. But, when the dust settles, one thing remains the same: they've got a scheme to make you rich, and all you have to do is send them a cashier's check.

One final note on their presentation. The caller will, in a matter of seconds, size you up and be able to tailor their fraud to your reservations. Make no mistake, these people can sell. Just how good are they? Many make over a million dollars a year, working a few hours a day. Others work as a crew. They travel from city to city, always one step ahead of the law. They are, for all intents, virtually unstoppable, as, by moving from county to county, state to state, they often become immune from jurisdiction where the offense(s) occurred, which is why many boiler room operations have been shut down only to reopen in a new location a few days later.

It should be mentioned that if you own a small business you are also likely to be a fraud target. Con-artists don't usually bother big business, as they have purchasing departments which know the routine all too well. The small business rip-off usually involves supplies for machinery or advertising in publications of questionable or non-existent groups. Regardless of the form, the telemarketer appeals to your greed.

Agencies that offer assistance if you're involved in a telemarketing fraud:

1. Federal Trade Commission
Office of Investment Fraud
Washington, DC 20580
202-523-3598

2. Securities & Exchange Commission
450 Fifth Street, N.W.
Washington, DC 20549
202-272-2650

3. State Attorney General's Office
(Check your phone book)

While these agencies can offer aid, your best defense is, if you receive a phone call from a person you don't know, and they try and sell you anything, hang up. It's really that simple.

YOUR CAR

DON'T BUY A NEW CAR

You'll save substantial money if you never buy a new car. That's always been true, but now more than ever, as new cars have price tags that make them prohibitive. It's not unusual to spend eighteen thousand dollars on a mid-size family car. And that doesn't include the finance charge associated with the purchase. That's why you must consider a used car whenever you buy a car. They make more common and economic sense.

The principle monetary problem with new cars, over and above their cost, is the fact that they depreciate so rapidly. The following chart makes the point.

Percentage Depreciation for Most New Cars:

First Year	30%
Second Year	25%
Third Year	20%
Fourth Year	15%
Fifth Year	10%

Sadly, the chart makes apparent that most American made cars have no monetary or lending value after five years. If you doubt that, check with your bank or the Blue or Black Book.

Let's take, as an example, that eighteen thousand dollar car I mentioned previously and apply the depreciation schedule to see the rapid decline in dollar value.

Dollar Depreciation for an $18,000 Car:

| End of First Year | $12,600.00 |
| End of Second Year | 8,100.00 |

End of Third Year	4,500.00
End of Fourth Year	1,800.00
End of Fifth Year	.00

While these numbers are rather alarming on their face, they also point up other areas of concern. For instance, if you sell this car after two years, your cost per year was $4,950.00 ($18,000 - $8,100 divided by 2). If you had sold at the end of the first year, your cost would have been $5,400.00 per year. That's quite a bit, especially since these figures simply reflect value depreciation and do not include gas, oil, maintenance, and insurance.

Now we get to the real bad news. Most of us have to finance a new car, and that adds dramatically to the cost. Here is typical financing for our example car.

Cost of Car	$18,000.00
Minus downpayment of 20%	3,600.00
Amount Financed	14,400.00
Credit Life & Disability Insurance	1,400.00
Total Financed	$15,800.00
Finance Charge (48 months at 9.5% add-on interest rate).	6,004.00
Total Loan	$21,804.00

(Note: You should never buy credit life & disability insurance. That notwithstanding, this is the typical method of financing for most new car buyers.)

See what a problem this financing, that we all probably need, causes? First, it increases what you paid for the car. In this case your true cost jumps to $25,404.00 ($21,804.00 plus your downpayment of $3,600.00). That's 41% over retail.

As most mid-size cars are marked up 16%, the wholesale value of the new car is only $15,480.00. The alarming bottomline here is that you paid 64% over wholesale!

When you add in the financing costs of an already overpriced new car, you have an economic disaster.

By now you have probably come to the conclusion that is my point: It is far better to buy a one or two-year-old used car than it is to buy a new car. Remember, a new car loses 55% of its value in the first two years, even though it maintains approximately 60% of its loan value. Its useful life is, in most instances, an even greater percentage.

To be fair, it has to be said that a used car may have some problems that need to be fixed. Additionally, except in rare instances, the warranty is probably no longer in effect. But, with the savings you accrue by buying a late model used car, you can afford a great deal in repairs. In fact, you could probably drop in a new engine and still be money ahead, because the costs associated with the first two years of a car's life cycle are so costly. The cost of driving our new car example per year is $3,600.00 (if you hold on to it for five years). The cost of driving that same car the last three years (assuming you buy it when it is two years old) is $2,700.00 per year. That's an up-front savings of $900.00 per year. And that doesn't include the substantially reduced financing costs. Nor the reduction in insurance expense.

I recommend that you always use a mechanic you trust to inspect your used car choice. Buying right is important, both in purchase price and later reductions in repair costs.

While this isn't a how-to for the actual car purchase, I want to mention this important tip: for the same used car, you'll pay the highest price to a new car dealer of the same make, less to a new car dealer of a differing make, even less to a used car dealer, and the bottom price to a private party.

The art of purchasing quality low-cost transporation has always been a worthy undertaking. Now it's a necessity. The cost of new cars has reached the point where, until recently, for the same price you could have purchased a small home.

That's why you have to consider alternatives. And the best alternative is buying a late model used car. The total cumulative savings, over the course of your financial lifetime, will, at today's rates, approximate sixty to seventy-thousand dollars. If costs keep escalating, as they most assuredly will, your savings will exceed even that.

USED CAR GUIDE

Regardless of your financial status, considering a used car makes sense from a bottomline perspective. Of course, there are some of us who have no choice but to consider a used car, as new car prices have reached a point beyond the means of many.

Assuming you, for whatever reason, are in the market for a good used car, how do you know if you're making a wise purchase?

First, you must, after accomplishing the following, understand the necessity of having the vehicle checked by an expert mechanic, someone not tied in any manner to the seller. Usually the cost for this service is less than $50 — cheap when you consider what his expertise may save you in repair charges. But, you can't afford to run to a mechanic with every car you are remotely interested in, as that could get expensive quickly. No, you only want to employ his service once you've located a car that can pass the following review:

1. LOOK AT THE CAR IN DAYLIGHT. The night covers too many warning signs that might otherwise be noticed immediately. Also, if it's raining, be aware even weather-beaten paint looks good when wet.

2. CHECK THE TIRES CLOSELY. If they're not evenly worn it indicates steering or balancing problems. Badly worn tires, besides being costly to replace, may indicate hard driving by the previous owner.

3. INSIST ON A TEST DRIVE. This sounds obvious, but many times the buyer only drives with the seller, which doesn't allow for a true feel of the car.

4. LOOK UNDER THE CAR. Don't let the seller bring the car to you. You want to look at the ground underneath the car while it's parked. If you see any fluid or fluid stains, watch out.

5. PRIOR TO TURNING ON THE CAR, RUN YOUR FINGER INSIDE THE EXHAUST PIPE. A black and/or oily residue means trouble, maybe an expensive valve job.

Have the seller start the car and look at the exhaust. If you have thick smoke, black or blue, you've probably got compression or carburetor trouble, both of which can be expensive.

6. LET THE CAR IDLE FOR AT LEAST 10 MINUTES. Turn on the air conditioner at max-cold. This will tell you if the car is prone to overheating. While you're waiting, check all the electrical devices; i.e., windshield wipers, radio, heater, and lights.

7. PUT ON THE PARKING BRAKE, PUT THE CAR IN DRIVE, AND CAREFULLY ACCELERATE. If the car doesn't quit, or almost quit, you may have faulty brakes or a transmission that needs repair.

8. LEAN ON THE CAR FROM ALL ANGLES. Push down hard and quickly on all corners. If the car bounces more than once, you'll be needing shocks.

From each corner, push hard to the side. If the car rocks back and forth badly, it may have been hit at one time.

9. SLAM ON THE BRAKES. During your test drive, at a moment when it's safe, slam on the brakes from a fairly high rate of speed. If the car pulls to one side or the other, you've got brake problems.

10. LET GO OF THE WHEEL. Again, at a time when safe, let go of the steering wheel. If the car steers to one side, you probably will need a realignment.

11. TEST DRIVE IN ALL CONDITIONS. Don't just drive slowly around town. You need to know if the car performs well at higher speeds, like those you'll be experiencing when you travel on a freeway. The car should respond satisfactorily under all driving conditions.

12. TEST RAPID ACCELERATION from a dead stop and while driving. Lack of response, at a minimum, indicates the need for a tune-up. At worst, it could mean the engine is shot.

If you're buying from a car dealer, you have to be aware of a number of tricks-of-the-trade which are routinely employed. That's not to insinuate they are practiced by all, but you have to be aware of what you might be up against.

1. CHECK THE PAINT. In this regard we're not concerned with simple appearances, or the look of the car. You should be searching for paint that doesn't appear to match, raising concern that the car has been hit and repaired.

2. CHECK THE METAL. Bring a small magnet with you and see if it sticks to the entire car. When you reach a part where the magnet falls, you are looking at a plastic repair covering rust or an accident.

3. LOOK AT THE SEAMS. Look down the trim line, the door lines, the hood line, etc. If they're wavy, the car has probably been hit.

4. BE WARY OF CARS THAT ARE TOO CLEAN. Check the engine. Is it super clean? That may be because, to cover various leakages, the seller steamed the engine.

Look under the car. Is it super clean? New undercoating is often used to cover rust or telltale accident signs.

5. LOOK FOR PAINT RESIDUE. Check the windows and chrome. If you see any paint spray watch out. They're trying to hide something.

When buying from a dealer, I strongly suggest that you take the time to contact the prior owner (his or her name can be found by looking at the title). This is an excellent way to ascertain that the mileage hasn't been tampered with, that the car hasn't been hit, the engine was running well at the time it was sold, etc. Previous owners usually will tell you all you need to know to verify the results of your inspection.

These pretests/cautions will indicate whether or not you should take the car to your mechanic. He will then proceed with reviewing the big ticket items that require knowledge and experience. He will, with as much certainty as humanly possible, ensure you're getting a fair deal. Of course, the obvious must be mentioned: even the best used car can have trouble the day after you buy it. But, the same thing can be said for many new cars.

My intent is to give you enough information for you to benefit from the financial rewards offered by buying a good used car. You can save money up-front, lower your insurance costs, and reduce your per-mile expense. All you have to do is take your time, apply my test(s), and take the car to a mechanic you trust implicitly.

SAVING YOUR CAR BUYING DOLLAR

Almost every one shops around for a car. It's not the kind of purchase you make on impulse. That's good. You should comparison shop for everything, as the savings can be immense. In the case of a car, new or used, we go to greater lengths than normal because we are aware of the rising cost of automobiles. We are also aware that the mark-up is substantial, which means there is negotiating room.

The bottomline on the purchase is that most of us are pretty sure we made the best deal possible no matter what car we bought. We shopped the options, we dissected the sticker, we haggled with the salesman, etc. We may have spent weeks or months making up our minds and arriving at the right new car price or finding the perfect used car. Again, all of this shopper dedication is to be applauded.

Then things start to unravel. The same people who spent time, money, and effort to get the best deal on the car of their choice usually forget an equally, if not more important aspect of car buying. The financing. Let's look at two examples:

1. DEALER FINANCING. Roughly half of all cars bought are dealer financed.

That means the dealership took your credit application and arranged your financing through a local area bank, or through a subsidiary of their car manufacturer.

First the bank financing. That scenario goes something like this. You feel comfortable because, as the salesman says, you will be financed by the local bank. You can't do better than that, right? And besides, you won't have to be bothered going downtown and filling out all those forms. They can do it all right there and they can do it faster. And, of course, it won't cost you any more than you could arrange yourself. On its face, that doesn't sound too bad, does it? Unfortunately, things aren't that simple.

Arranged financing from a dealer to a bank means one thing and one thing only. It's going to cost you more than it should to acquire what you could have received on your own. It works like this. Everything the salesman told you is correct, except for one important point. Your financing rate includes a bank to dealer kickback that may be anywhere from 1 to 4 percentage points additional interest on the loan.

Let's use an example to make the point of how costly this can become. On a $10,000.00 loan for 48 months, this means unnecessary costs to you of $400.00 to $1,600.00. You'll never know that because it won't be on your loan documentation. You'll just see a rate and an amount. You'll never know what portion belongs to the bank and what portion belongs to the dealer. I object to this bank/dealer relationship because the customer is being deceived and cannot make an intelligent financial decision. Meaning, they are about to lose money.

Particularly distressing here is the bank's part in this deception. Many of you may have allowed your dealer to arrange financing at your bank; i.e., the bank where you do all your personal banking. You'd think a local bank would at least protect their customers! Not so. Instead of helping you keep your costs down, they, more than likely, helped the dealer take more of your money. The bank could have made you a direct loan at X%, but, because you allowed the dealer to arrange the financing, you got charged X plus %. Your bank sold you out. This happens in almost every community, as virtually all banks have some car dealer relationships.

The point is, just because your or another local bank is involved doesn't mean you're getting a good deal by letting the dealer arrange financing.

2. THE 1.9% COME-ON. One of the more deceptive practices new car dealerships are presently participating in is promotion of very low interest rate financing come-on's.

These were started by the manufacturers in answer to lagging domestic car sales; since they could no longer sell the product, they would sell the financing. What could possibly be wrong with 1.9% financing? A lot.

First of all, that rate may only apply for a few months on a few models. You have to ensure the rate applies to what you're interested in. You will, if you're not careful, be a victim of a very clever bait-and-switch.

Also, because dealers have you thinking interest rate, you may forget the car. Everything sounds so good, the dealer takes advantage of other ways to make money. For instance, they sell you credit life and disability insurance in the financing. They sell you a worthless extended warranty. They talk you into their answer to rust coating. Any one of these or other items will more than off-set your savings of the lower interest rate.

More importantly, most dealers will not negotiate the car price itself, because of the lower interest rate. They will say things like, "At these rates I don't have any room to negotiate." Of course, that's nonsense. The financing rate through the manufacturer and the cost of the car are two entirely separate things. One does not affect the other, but the dealer will try and convince you they are intertwined. That means there are substantial rip-offs in the sticker price. Things like inflated mark-ups, delivery, preparation, etc. These are big income producers to the dealer — and big unnecessary losses for you.

Here too, if the dealer can get you thinking interest rate, he can sell you a car at a very inflated price.

Buying a car is an expensive proposition, and it's getting more expensive all the time. That means the sales techniques employed by dealers and/or manufacturers are going to get more and more clever in an attempt to hide from you that the car itself may be poorly made and overpriced.

It should be mentioned, in fairness, that low rate financing deals can be a good buy, provided you demand all the concessions you normally would when buying a car. Don't stop haggling because the financing rate is low. Don't buy worthless insurances and/or substandard rust proofing, etc. Don't buy at a dealership just because they advertised a low rate of X%, if it doesn't pertain to you because of term or the car you are buying.

There are good car dealerships; not many, but they're there. Unfortunately, I'm afraid, as the market gets tougher and tougher, it will be harder and harder to find a fair deal anywhere. That means your shopping has to become more demanding than ever. The dealers will attack you on two fronts. First they want to overprice the product. Then they want to make additional monies on the financing.

You, as an informed buyer, can beat them at their own game.

YOUR TAXES

LOWER YOUR INCOME TAX

You must employ a tax expert. Why? In 1930 the average person could pay their tax obligation with 40 days work. Today, even with so-called tax reform, you have to work 122 days to pay your taxes. That amounts to 47% of your available work days to pay your tax bill. This may sound impossible, but, sadly, it's not. Bringing matters into focus, add up your federal, state, sales, gas, real estate, city, and Social Security taxes. The total drives home the point — you have to try and avoid taxes.

Taxes are a financial burden only for the middle class. The poor don't pay taxes. Neither do the super rich. The affluent know an important, money saving truth: tax evasion is illegal — avoidance isn't. There is a fine line here, but one that is workable. Supreme Court Justice Felix Franfurter said, "As to the astuteness of taxpayers in ordering their affairs as to minimize taxes, we have said that, 'The very meaning of a line in the law is that you may intentionally go as close to it as you can if you do not pass it'. This is so because nobody owes any public duty to pay more than the law demands. Taxes are enforced extractions, not voluntary contributions."

Most of us never realize the distinction between tax evasion and avoidance. Let's use an analogy. Tax avoidance is like shopping at a discount grocery store. Tax evasion is like stealing groceries. The contrast is obvious. So are the consequences. Unfortunately, the IRS has us so intimidated that too few avoid what taxes they can. If that includes you, you are a willing tax abuse participant. Believe me, the IRS doesn't need your assistance, they do quite well on their own.

Taxpayers erroneously believe as long as they don't rock the boat they will not have problems with the IRS. That's false. Congressional hearings make clear that innocent Americans have lived nightmares, and, in some cases, had complete financial destruction due to IRS mistreatment. Unfortunately, the average citizen, one who tries to cooperate with the IRS, stands a much better chance of being assaulted than someone truly guilty of breaking the tax laws; i.e., cooperation doesn't necessarily offer abatement. The IRS is staffed by human beings who have all the frailties, prejudices, bad days, misunderstandings, etc., we all have. Meaning, no matter how innocent, you may be at risk. Adding to that exposure, IRS exams are, in effect, processed under the unspoken guidelines of, "You're guilty until proven innocent."

Let's review this issue's bottomline. For all intents, the richest families and corporations pay no taxes, while you probably pay a third or more of your income to various taxing bodies. When you avoid taxes, which is your right, you help ensure fairness that might otherwise be denied.

There are many, many ways to avoid taxes. No matter what your financial status, you can probably reduce your obligation. It's foolish not to. I am amazed that most never make any substantive effort. They'll travel all over town trying to save fifty dollars on an appliance and then overpay the IRS thousands without a whimper. You should try and reduce all your expenses — including taxes. That means tax avoidance. And the way to exploit tax avoidance is to use the services of a professional, for two reasons. First and foremost, it reduces your expense. Secondly, if there is a problem, your expert will be there to take the IRS' heat. That's the way the financially elite beat our tax system — even though that system is designed to take as much of your hard earned money as possible. If the rich can avoid taxes, so can you.

Tax reform promised, among other things, tax simplification. That didn't happen. Tax reform promised fairness. That didn't happen either. But, that's old news. The matter at hand is that taxes are constantly raised for the majority of the middle class. Additionally, the tax code is becoming more and more complicated. Because of reform, and the events since, you are going to pay more taxes in sum total. There is no foreseeable respite from the constant federal, state, and local tax assault. Consequently, you are forced to be a tax expert or employ one. Yes, this will cost you, but a true expert should be able to save you their fee and more.

Let's assume that you follow my advice and hire a tax expert. The issue then becomes, how can you maximize his service at the lowest possible cost? Tax accountants charge either by filing or by the hour. For most, the hourly charge is the most cost-effective. You will want to reduce the accountant's time as much as possible, so you need to be organized before you walk into his or her office. Just because you have a tax accountant doesn't mean you don't have to do any work. Your accountant, if any good, will charge a substantial hourly wage. It would be a waste of money to have him perform clerical tasks you could have taken care of yourself.

Here's a list of things you should do prior to and/or bring to your appointment. You'll need to:

1. GATHER YOUR RECORDS. Take anything that might be important. It's better to be overprepared than have to go home during the appointment, or worse yet, have to reschedule to bring additional materials.

2. BRING A COMPLETE LISTING OF YOUR INCOME. This should include salary, dividends, rentals, interest, appropriate business gains or losses, etc. If you have two wage earners, bring documentation for both.

3. PROVIDE ALL STOCK AND SECURITIES DOCUMENTATION. Start with your monthly statements from your broker, or mutual fund, etc. It will help to sort them so everything flows and is easily understood. Just handing your accountant a pile of papers isn't the best idea. Remember, he will be billing on an hourly basis.

4. LIST EXPENSES. Who, what, where, when, and why not only works for reporters, it works with tax documentation. List your medical, business, interest, taxes, charitable

contributions, etc., and have the documentation that proves the expense.

If you're not sure of an item, bring it anyway. Assume it's deductible until you're told otherwise.

5. OFFER REAL ESTATE DOCUMENTS. All title reports, closing statements, lawyers bills, bank statements, etc., for any real estate sales or purchases made during the year should be included for review.

6. DOCUMENT ESTIMATED TAX PAYMENTS. If you've paid any estimated tax, bring statements and supporting cancelled checks.

If you're starting out with a new accountant, ask him, before your appointment, how many prior year's returns he would like to see. Most like to review a minimum of three years.

Inquire if there is anything else he might need. Depending on your particulars, he may have additional, seemingly unusual requirements. Again, ask first. Accountants get busy and don't think of things until the last moment, especially around tax time, so take it upon yourself to ensure your meeting is productive. Some tax professionals mail clients an outline that catalogs their needs (a sign they probably know what they're doing.)

While on the subject of tax accountants/lawyers, it is usually more profitable to use their services all year, as opposed to just tax preparation. Take advantage of money saving tax planning advice. Consider this all-encompassing approach regardless of your economic station. Tax planning is another subject, but it affects this section because the tax code is so confusing even the IRS can't explain it.

The best way to be able to provide the information and documentation your accountant demands is to have an ongoing tax record-keeping system. Don't wait until a few days before the filing deadline to start running around trying to decipher what you did all year with your money. Devise whatever filing method you find comfortable. Regardless of form, spend a little time every month keeping it up to date. It doesn't take long and the amount of time you spend each month will add up to far less than what you'll have to spend if you wait until the end of the year. It is easier to keep current than it is to reconstruct twelve months of financial activity. If you have a computer, there are fairly inexpensive tax/bookkeeping software programs available. At the other end of the spectrum, a lot of very wealthy people use envelopes for each income and expense category, and then those envelopes are filed in a shoe box. It doesn't matter how sophisticated, as long as it gets done.

To focus this important issue, it should be said again, truly wealthy people don't pay taxes. One part of their plan to become wealthy was paying as little tax as possible along the way. You can learn from their success.

AVOIDING TAX AUDITS

No matter how honest you are, or how thoroughly you've prepared your tax return, if you receive notice of an IRS audit, you're probably going to be concerned. And if you're not, you should be, because the tax laws are so confused that if the IRS examiner wants to find a violation in your return, he can. That puts us all at risk, and strongly indicates you should do whatever necessary to decrease your odds of an audit.

What are your odds of getting audited?

Income	Audits
$10,000 to 25,000 (itemized)	1.68%
$10,000 to 25,000 (not itemized)	.65%
$25,000 to 50,000	2.03%
Over $50,000	3.52%

If you're self-employed, your odds increase dramatically:

Under $25,000	1.45%
$25,000 to 100,000	2.57%
Over $100,000	5.42%

If your audit turns up any information that the agent feels deserves further scrutiny, your audit may turn into an investigation. IRS's investigations are broken down as follows:

Individuals	58.2%
Business owners	23.1%
Business executives	5.4%
Corporate officers	4.9%
Attorneys	3.5%

Professionals (doctors, etc.)	2.2%
Accountants	1.8%
CPA's	.9%

Approximately 18% of investigations end in actual prosecution. The results of that litigation are as follows:

Cases

For taxpayer	21%
For IRS	59%
Split decisions	20%

Appeals

For taxpayer	24.0%
For IRS	71.5%
Split decisions	4.5%

(The above percentages are drawn from the Annual Report of the IRS.)

The best way to reduce your chances of being part of these statistics is to avoid drawing attention to your return. How? By circumventing certain items that immediately draw additional IRS inspection. You should also avoid presenting information that doesn't make sense.

Specifically:

1. As strange as this may sound, the earlier you file your return, the better the odds that you will be audited. Common sense would indicate just the opposite, but since audits have to be scheduled within the time resources of IRS field offices, the quicker they have your figures, the more time they have to include you in their plans.

2. You should answer all questions on your return. If you overlook some, even if the answer would

have been no, the examiners will be drawn to reviewing the entire return.

3. Make a professional presentation. If you're sloppy on the form, they often assume you're sloppy with your numbers too.

4. If you have a tax preparer, make sure their reputation is above question. If your accountant is in trouble with the IRS, so are you.

5. Specifically identify all your income. Avoid categories like "Other Income." Spell it out on your 1040 or your examiner will ask you to prove it face-to-face. The same holds true for expenses. Words like miscellaneous are a red flag to an IRS staff person.

6. Avoid questionable tax shelters. Some shelters are still legal, but be careful. Don't assume that the seller of the shelter was telling the truth when they assured you of its IRS acceptability. Make sure you have proof before investing.

7. Don't round-off or estimate your figures. Your return should be accurate to the penny.

8. Make sure your return is intact. Don't send a lot of loose forms, because something may get lost along the way. Missing schedules automatically mean, at the very least, you are going to be contacted.

9. Ensure your math is correct. This sounds so simple, but it is the most common error found on tax returns.

10. Avoid making common sense mistakes. For example, you list the sale of stock that pays dividends, but your return lists no dividend income. Or you're married, but file separate returns, and both take a few of the same deductions. There are many oversights like this that can immediately trigger an audit.

11. If you're self-employed, you should itemize your personal return. Why? Because the IRS sometimes assumes that you're charging personal expenses to the business if you take the standard deduction on your personal return.

12. Match your deductions to your income. If you're a middle income person by salary, you'd better not have affluent deductions.

13. While you obviously must avoid owing monies at year end, you must also ensure that your refund isn't too large. Large refunds trigger suspicion. From another angle, why would you want this situation in the first place, as you should want the government to use as little of your money as legally possible.

14. Lastly, while it is not possible to give an all-inclusive listing, any gaps can be covered by saying you must remember that IRS employees are human. After your return is complete, review it from their perspective. Apply a common sense value judgement to your tax presentation. See anything out of line? Anything look suspicious? If you feel the slightest bit skeptical, I can assure you that the IRS will feel likewise.

There are other factors influencing your odds of being audited that you should be aware of. For instance, if you live in a city, you are much more likely to be an audit recipient than if you live in a rural area. If you live in a big city, your odds escalate even further.

You may be at additional risk due to your profession. Doctors, dentists, auto salesmen, teachers, pilots, waitresses, and cab drivers are some of those the IRS looks at more closely than others.

It is imperative that you prepare, or cause to have prepared, a completely honest tax return. However, just because you do doesn't mean you won't be audited. And, as millions of people can tell you, an IRS audit is something you can live without. Even assuming that the audit reveals nothing to your detriment, it is something you want to avoid.

The best way to accomplish that goal is to understand how the IRS processes returns that subsequently receive further attention. Excluding dishonest returns, the majority of audits are caused by either the luck of the draw, i.e., you are randomly picked through the computer-generated audit program, or the taxpayer makes a mistake that could have avoided. That's the area I'm concerned with. It's bad enough if you get audited. It's absurd if you caused the irritation by making a small mistake or honest error that could have been avoided.

The bottomline is this. You can either spend a few extra hours preparing your tax return or you can spend days, weeks, or months explaining it to an IRS agent. My guidelines will substantially reduce the odds of the latter.

IRS AUDITS

Almost everyone is afraid of the Internal Revenue Service (IRS). They, probably more than any other government agency, have mastered the fine art of intimidation. That works to their favor and advantage.

That intimidation is never so clear as when they exercise their right to audit. It doesn't matter whether the audit is being completed on an individual or the nation's largest business, the dread and fear level is about the same. Why? It's not that taxpayers are worried that they are going to be "caught." Most of us pay our taxes correctly and, in fact, most of us overpay our taxes due to confusion and misunderstanding of the code.

Most fear an IRS audit because they don't understand the system, and, at least subconsciously, they know it is possible that they made one or more honest mistakes on their return. The fact is, if IRS examiners want to find an error on any return, they can. The code is that confusing and open to subjectivity.

Strip away all the tinsel and what you have is the IRS admitting through their actions that no one, not even their employees, knows how to interpret the tax code. That is even worse now, with the Tax Reform Act of 1986. That's why an audit strikes fear in the hearts of even the most honest among us. If the IRS wants to cause you trouble, they can. If they want to find an error, they will. That's not to say that IRS examiners are not dedicated, honest individuals, because most are. But, that's not the point. Subjectivity is dangerous, and our tax code is open to interpretation. That means you are at risk during an audit.

The IRS came into existence through the 16th Amendment, which says, "The Congress shall have the power to lay and collect taxes on incomes, from whatever source derived, without apportionment among the several states, without regard to any census or enumeration." It was ratified February 25, 1913.

On the subject of ratification, I found an interesting quote from Richard E. Bird, speaking in the House of Delegates (Virginia), during the ratification debate. No matter what your feelings are regarding the tax code, I think you'll find his thoughts frighteningly accurate:

"An army of federal inspectors, spies and detectives will descend upon the state. They will compel men of business to show their books and disclose the secrets of their affairs. They will dictate forms of bookkeeping. They will require statements and affidavits. On the one hand, the inspector can blackmail the taxpayer and on the other, he can profit by selling his secret to his competitor.

"This amendment will do what the 14th and 15th Amendments did not do — it will extend the federal power source to reach the citizen in the ordinary business of life. A hand from Washington will be stretched out and placed upon every man's business; the eye of the federal inspector will be in every man's counting house."

Delegate Bird, at least on this subject, was brilliant.

To cope with the tax code in its entirety, learn to live with it in its worst form, the audit.

The vast majority of audits are generated by a mistake in simple arithmetic, or because the taxpayer didn't use the proper form(s). That's another good reason to have a tax expert doing your return. Other returns are audited because the return fell outside acceptable computer model parameters. This too could be avoided by using an expert, as they usually know exactly what the parameters are, and they will seldom exceed them.

As much as I don't like the implication, I have to bring to your attention that many returns (especially those of businesses) are audited because someone informed the IRS that they thought Mr. X or Company X was cheating. In some cases, the IRS is willing to pay the informant for the information and/or a portion of the additional tax collected.

You should also be aware that in this age of computers and subsequent cross checking, you must not forget a single

penny of income. There are many entities reporting to the
IRS, and all that information is matched to your return. If
something comes up tilt, you most assuredly will be audited,
so exercise caution in compiling your documentation.

Lastly, on this aspect, you have to be aware that your
return may have been picked for scrutiny simply at random.
There's not much you can do about the luck of the draw.
Random checking is increasing every year as computers become more sophisticated. That unfortunately means your
chances of winning the IRS-audit-lottery are getting better.
Another reason why you should employ an expert.

IRS audits fall into two categories — civil and criminal.
The vast majority fall into the former, and the agent is simply concerned with collecting money and perhaps assessing a
few penalties. There are times, however, when a civil audit
turns into a criminal audit, but hopefully that will not be
germane to my readers.

The criminal audit is usually processed by a special or
intelligence agent. If your audit agent introduces himself
with one of those titles (or you find out he has that title), you
have a problem and should immediately ask to see your attorney. Say nothing without counsel.

While you actually have little to fear during an audit,
assuming you have done nothing illegal, it still pays to exercise caution. Remember, the tax code is partially subjective,
which means the impression of illegality can cause trouble
even if none was attempted. Of course, the best way not to
let your audit degenerate to the danger point is not to deal
with the examiner directly. Have your accountant or lawyer
handle the audit. That way you won't say anything that can
be misunderstood. Again, the employment of an expert will
be worth the expense.

On the subject of the actual audit, it needs to be said
that many audits are brought on by the taxpayer; i.e., they
focused attention on themselves and now have to pay the
penalty. To the point, if you constantly ask for extensions,
file amended returns, and write complaining letters, you

have substantially increased your odds of an audit. One of the best ways to avoid an audit is to limit your IRS contact. Use some common sense and remain as inconspicuous as possible.

You have numerous rights during an audit and should avail yourself of same when necessary. Remember, that agent is human too, and that means the more you antagonize him or her, the less your chances that you'll be pleased with the result. However, it should also be noted that the very notice of an audit means we have an adversary relationship up-front. They're not coming out to tell you how pleased they were with your filing. So, be prepared, and try to walk the fine line between protecting your interests and helping the agent.

You probably will not need the following, especially if you have your accountant or lawyer handle the audit, but I want you to have this information available nonetheless:

1. You have the right against self-incrimination, which in this case means you don't have to give up your records if you believe they will send you to jail.

2. You have the right to be treated with respect and dignity, and are not to be subjected to abuse of any kind.

3. You have a right to be represented by counsel and/or your accounting experts (as outlined by IRS rulings).

4. You have a right to notice of the audit; i.e., the agent hasn't the right to show up out of the blue and demand your records. You can decline if that happens, and then set up a meeting at a later date.

5. You have a right to decide where the audit will take place. You can deny the examiner the right to conduct the audit at your house or place of business. If it will better meet your needs, ask to have the audit conducted at the IRS office.

6. You have a right to protect your property from search and seizure unless served with a warrant, so don't let things get out of hand or allow the agent the right to go on a fishing expedition.

7. You have the right to be protected from harassment. You cannot be examined, re-examined, re-re-examined, and so on. Your lawyer can help you here. They will call this protection into play long before you will.

8. You have the right to attorney/client privilege. That means, if you give all your records to your attorney for assistance with an audit, they cannot be indiscriminately seized by the IRS. Those records become part of the attorney/client privilege and, as such, cannot be abused. This right is not valid in relationship to your accountant.

9. You have the right, no matter what the findings of the audit, to appeal. There are numerous appeal outlets, depending on the severity of the problem.

No one looks forward to an IRS audit, but it doesn't have to be the end of the world. In fact, it could be something quite simple. It may not even involve money, or perhaps a very small amount. Clearly, understanding the system, and making allowances for the agent's state of mind will help your audit procedure. Following my advice, before the fact, may help insure you never have an audit, which would be the ideal circumstance.

Regardless, understand this, your chances of experiencing an audit are increasing due to technology. That makes it incumbent on you to employ a tax expert. Of course, they don't work cheap but this is one area where you have to spend money to make or save money. A good tax expert will save you enough in taxes to pay for their services. If they don't, fire them.

Finally, in an attempt to set your mind at ease, this country doesn't have a debtor prison. Almost any IRS/tax problem can be worked out.

YOUR INVESTMENTS

THE TRUTH ABOUT STOCKBROKERS

I have a very low opinion of stockbrokers. Why? Because they're deceitful. They masquerade as objective financial advisors when they're nothing more than salesman. This observation isn't conjecture, it's a conclusion based on the industry itself. Brokers earn management plaudits not by obtaining profits for their clients, but for the profit they earn the house. The more they sell, the more "successful" they become — regardless if their clients lose their shirts.

That's why I advise using the financial services of an independent broker, one who doesn't profit from sales commissions or have a relationship with another that may be harmful to you. Often, when one thinks they have found unbiased advice, they are mistaken. For example, when you purchase one of the major financial magazines, it probably doesn't occur to you that their objectivity is highly suspect. There are advertising revenues to consider. If they have a big advertiser, like a representative of the banking industry, are they going to print a story highly critical of banks? Unlikely. In fact, in some cases they may offer the advertiser solace by printing a positive article in their time of need. The problem is, the unsuspecting reader never understands the motivation of a slanted story. The potential for damaging investment consequences is great.

There are other instances when things are not what they seem. Financial planners are a perfect example. Unbeknownst to most, almost 80% of financial planners are paid on commission. In short, they're just like most stockbrokers.

How valuable is having an objective source for financial advice? Let's look at four disturbing truths about stockbrokers:

1. MANY BROKERS ARE SALES PEOPLE HIRED FROM OTHER INDUSTRIES. As shocking as that sounds, it's true. Very few brokers have the educational background in securities you'd expect. They were hired because they were successful salespeople at their former job, which may have been insurance, telephone, or used car sales.

2. BROKERS ARE PAID TO SELL. Stockbrokers who sell the most get paid the most. Although this was mentioned above, it has to be repeated, as it severely sullies the advisor/client relationship.

In addition to their commissioned salaries, brokers are paid bonuses for being the top salesman of the month, quarter, or year. Sadly, to my knowledge, there isn't one brokerage house that rewards their staff for the profit they generate their clients.

3. BROKERAGE RESEARCH IS WORTHLESS. Every independent survey I've encountered makes clear that basing investment decisions on recommendations of a brokerage house is a huge mistake. When compared to other information sources, brokerage houses usually score in the bottom half in terms of accuracy. Unfortunately, because of facade, individual investors believe brokerage house research recommendations. Seldom do they ascertain if the house has a worthy track record.

While we're on the subject of brokerage house research departments, when's the last time your broker called with a sell recommendation? This seldom occurs because the house or broker doesn't want to offend the company that would be the unfortunate target of that advice. The company's management may have other business with the house, business the house would lose if it told its clients to sell. This is another case of cross-purpose, hidden interests that should cause you to question your broker relationship.

4. BROKERS OFTEN PUSH VERY RISKY INVESTMENTS. Too often, brokers make every effort to entice clients to buy extremely risky investments. Why? Once again, it's personal, commissioned profits.

The broker's commission is not the same for each investment. Usually, the higher the risk, the higher the commission. New issues, speculative stocks, and in-house mutual funds are but a few examples of potentially unsafe investments that return the broker a higher commission.

Conservative investments, like T-bills, mutual funds, and bank CDs earn the broker little or nothing. When was the last time your broker recommended one of these safe investments? Probably never.

You should invest in vehicles offering a known degree of safety. Of course, there's an element of risk in every investment. Notwithstanding, there is a fundamental wrong in a system that pushes and then rewards brokers, supposed people of trust, to sell their clients the largest amount of the riskiest investment the house offers.

Investing is a difficult undertaking even when all things are equal. When the playing field is tipped, it's almost impossible. Brokers, the people most of us turn to for market advice, are the very people who have the most to gain by selling you something you don't need. There is a two point solution to the problem:

1. GET YOUR INVESTMENT ADVICE FROM AN INDEPENDENT. You should expect to pay a reasonable fee for their advice, because good investment counsel isn't cheap. More important than price is objectivity — as soon as there is any form of commission involved a broker's opinion can't be trusted.

2. OPEN A DISCOUNT BROKERAGE ACCOUNT. If you really need the assistance of a full-service broker, you probably shouldn't be in the market.

Over and above the immense savings of a discount account (you can save as much as 70% on each trade — a moderately active investor can save over $50,000 in commissions during their lifetime), it will sever the dangerous, dependent relationship you may have had with your previous broker.

The truth about stockbrokers isn't pretty. It's become so negative that many houses, in an attempt to evade the taint, now call their brokers consultants, account representatives, or whatever other pleasant sounding euphemism they can think of. They can try and hide, but it won't work. No matter what they're called, they're salesmen — salesmen encouraged and paid to take as much of your money they can.

PERSONAL FINANCIAL PLANNING

One characteristic that appears to be universal among affluent people is they never allow themselves to lose hands-on control of their finances. That fact is diametrically contrary to the reality that the average investor does just the opposite.

That's why there are brokers, financial planners, investment bankers, advisors, etc. Investors are looking for an easy way to riches. They want someone else to take them by the hand and do all the work, while they reap the benefits. The truth be told, there are no benefits. If there were, everyone who has a broker would be rich, and we know that's not true. The so-called experts are nothing more than salesmen. They get rich selling advice. Unfortunately their clients don't get rich using that advice. That's the bottomline. And yet, hundreds of millions of dollars are spent every year by investors looking for the latest hot tip or technique.

You and you alone are equipped to charter your financial future. Granted, you can seek advice and make it a part of your plan, but past that it is foolish to assume that someone else is going to make you rich. Let's look at the reason that's not going to happen:

1. THERE IS NO MODEL INVESTOR. What's good for one is not good for another. Yet that's what most advisers offer, general, generic advice. Dangerous and disappointing results occur when one follows generalities.

2. THERE IS NO MODEL PORTFOLIO. Each investor has different needs and expectations. What's right for a young family of four can't be right for an elderly retired couple. Unfortunately, people at far ends of the financial spectrum are often listening and following the advice of the same "expert(s)." In this scenario, the chances of success are minimal.

3. THERE IS NO MODEL INVESTMENT. There are approximately fifty thousand stocks, two hundred mutual funds, TCDs, bonds, real estate, collectibles, personal lend-

ing, etc., and each has merit. With all the present investment opportunities, it would be foolish to assume that anyone not familiar with your specific, intimate, personal finances could offer direction and/or advice that would produce the kind of results you deserve.

4. WHAT IS GOOD ADVICE TODAY MAY BE BAD ADVICE TOMORROW. That's why you have to be on top of your game at all times. Unfortunately, many experts have one position and one position only. They sell stocks. They sell real estate. They sell mutual funds. They sell rare coins. You get the idea. The single vision technique they offer will occasionally produce profits, but overall you'll be the poorer for their advice. Why? Once again, they're salesmen. Nothing more, nothing less.

These are just a few of the reasons you must rely on yourself for financial planning. You're the only one who has something to lose. Let's look at it another way. When's the last time your broker lost money dealing with you? Your insurance agent? Estate planner? Your mutual fund? Your banker? Your investment service? The point is, they make money every time you transact business. Can you say the same?

It should be said at this juncture that personal financial planning is not something most of us like to do, at least not the way it should be done. It's not easy and it takes time. It must take into consideration all aspects of the equation — your capital, needs, expectations, liquidity, and goals — which you have to adapt to what is available at that moment. And this has to be done almost daily, as the market changes rapidly.

Let's look at some aspects you should review before making any decisions:

1. Garner as much information as you can assemble. Here's one area where outsiders can help. Use them for reference, which in most cases can be

culled at no expense. No informational opportunity should be missed for results to be maximized.

2. Once you put together your options, don't look only for the plusses of an investment, look for the negatives. Here's where many go wrong. They forget the bad news. Experts are good at this one-sided review. Up-side they know. Down-side they ignore. You can't afford such a limited appraisal. It's like the old analogy, "Some of the best trades in baseball are trades that were never made." The same holds true with investments. In many cases, after looking at all sides, doing nothing is the best move you can make.

3. Once you make an investment decision, step back and review it again. It may take minutes or days depending on the circumstances. Regardless, a re-review is almost always called for. The more you dissect an investment, the easier it will be to see it in its entirety. That's important. You can't afford to at some point have to say, "I never thought of that." Think before you invest. It's cheaper.

Are there technical aspects of personal investing that deserve specific attention? I believe there are. They are best explained by using examples of what my research shows is common among consistent investment winners:

1. INVESTMENT WINNERS ARE NEVER FULLY INVESTED. To do so would limit their options and reduce their ability to react to new opportunities.

2. THEY KNOW THE ENTIRE TRANSACTION MUST BE TAKEN INTO CONSIDERATION. That is, inflation, taxes, transaction costs, etc. You must see the net return of your investments.

3. WINNERS KNOW YOU MAKE PROFITABLE INVESTMENT DECISIONS BASED ON THE FACTS OF TODAY, NOT FUTURE PREDICTIONS. This today's-real-

ity approach will be right far more often than any prediction you or any expert can make. You'll find this approach right approximately 75% of the time. Does your Wall Street guru have a batting average approaching that?

4. THEY KNOW THE DETAILS OF EACH INVESTMENT. If they invest in a company's stock, they know the company, its inner workings, its realistically appraised future, and so on.

If they invest in gold, they know gold's cycles. They know assaying requirements/costs, storage costs, and potential saleability problems.

Any investment is only an investment if you understand all its ramifications. If you don't, you're speculating, not investing.

5. INVESTMENT WINNERS DON'T FORCE A BALANCE WITH THEIR HOLDING. That is, they don't make an investment and then see if it meets their needs. They verbalize their expectations and then search for the investment vehicle that will produce results to meet their goals.

6. THEY KNOW IT'S JUST AS IMPORTANT, IF NOT MORE SO, TO KNOW HOW TO GET OUT OF AN INVESTMENT AS IT IS TO GET INTO IT. Real estate is a perfect example of this point. It sounds good up front, but selling the property when you have other immediate, more pressing financial considerations can cause major losses. A winner knows this before the fact and anticipates the same when deciding whether or not to buy.

It's your money, it's your responsibility. Make the most of it. If you're depending on others, you'll end up with less than you could have had.

One has to ask why anyone would trust someone else, including the experts, with their family's financial future. To be successful, every relationship, including financial associations, must have balance. That's impossible when you are not your own financial planner. No one has as much to lose as you do.

Again, it makes sense to use professionals to gather information for your plan. That notwithstanding, you should make decisions on your own, even if you employ a financial planner.

Once you start this process, you'll find it easier than you imagine. Also, I have found most investors who act as their own decision makers tend to be more financially prudent than others they might rely on. Which, of course, will save you money.

Those who become their own financial planners quickly find out one other important fact of financial life: you're better than the experts.

10 BIG INVESTMENTS EVERYONE CAN AFFORD

Perhaps the biggest investment mistake made by those yet to be rich is not maximizing their return on every dollar. The reason for this error is probably born from the idea that to invest profitably you need a lot of money. While it's true that having ample resources helps, it should occur to most that, excluding those with inherited wealth, at one point in their life, affluent people were in the same boat you may be in now. And yet, they didn't let that stop them. They understood that you must invest, regardless of your financial station. Understanding your investment abilities while you're striving to become wealthy will determine whether you reach your goal.

When you're starting out, you have little you can afford to lose. Once you're wealthy, while you don't want to accept losses, you can afford them. That important consideration allows for an expansion of investment opportunities. Opportunities that, in addition to possible added risk, offer potential for outstanding rewards. But this section isn't about what you're going to do once you've made it. I'm concerned about how you're going to get there. And to accomplish that task, you have to realize ways to invest as if you had more money than you do. You have to ferret out options that offer potentially large rewards with small minimum investments.

1. MUTUAL FUNDS. Elsewhere in this book, I discuss the idea of mutual funds. How they offer important diversification, good to excellent returns, low or no fees, and low minimums (usually $100.00).

More important presently, due to the volatility of today's market, is the wide variety of funds available. There are growth funds, round lot stock funds, overseas investment funds (worth considering with the coming economic unification of Western Europe), bond funds, small company funds, tax free funds, zero-coupon Treasury funds, etc. For a complete listing of the better known/producing funds, pick up a copy of any financial monthly at a newsstand. The funds are listed, along with phone numbers to call for a prospectus. Mutual funds have never offered the wide diversification they do now. You can invest in the same blue chip investments and get the same returns as the big boys by using this important tool.

2. TIME CERTIFICATES OF DEPOSIT (TCDs). I am not normally in favor of financial institution investing. That notwithstanding, I draw your attention to times when rates have escalated to a plateau where this simplest of investments, a time certificate, or other financial institution vehicles, must be considered, to lock-in a lofty rate.

Of course, when rates do reach this position, you should rate shop your certificates; i.e., don't just run down to your local bank. Explore insured market TCDs. Oftentimes you can add X% over-and-above the rate offered by most financial institutions.

This important investment tool is recommendable only when rates are favorable to the saving consumer. But, if conditions warrant, you should take advantage of the opportunity.

3. BUY BLUE CHIP STOCKS. In my consulting I find that many people, when discussing blue chip stocks, would like to be able to afford to buy shares in some of the expensive, can't-miss winners. Now virtually anyone can. That kind of limited thinking is what keeps the less affluent less affluent. Virtually anyone can buy blue chips. Just buy fewer shares.

If you feel that high priced stock X is the right stock for you, buy it. Your return is relative, regardless of the number of shares owned. So if you're one of those who has ignored blue chips because you thought you couldn't afford them, think again.

4. MONEY MARKET ACCOUNTS. There are hundreds of billions of dollars sitting in banks throughout the country earning little or nothing. How much of your hard-earned cash does your bank have, and what are they paying you for the use of those funds?

Everyone should have an interest-rate-competitive money market account. And all you have to do to retrieve your money is make a phone call or write a check. Shop local area brokers and financial institutions for the best deal.

Cash is an asset, a valuable asset. Treat it like one. To make the point: $1,000.00 returning 10% over 40 years (an investor's average financial lifetime) compounds to $53,700.66. Do you have $1,000.00 you're not investing to the fullest?

5. BECOME A LENDER. Not many of us have the time, money, and expertise to lend to individuals. That's too bad because lending can offer extraordinary returns with little exposure to risk if the loan is structured properly. However, institutional lending opportunities still exist. For example, buy a corporate bond. They can usually be purchased for as little as $1,000.00. Call your broker. The returns can be excellent, and, assuming you verify the bond rating to ascertain the company's creditworthiness, risk is virtually non-existent.

These are almost always overlooked by small investors.

6. ZERO COUPON BONDS. Zero coupon bonds don't make scheduled interest payments. Instead they are sold at a discount and then, when redeemed, are done so at full face value.

Zeros can fluctuate in value if you have to sell prior to maturity, but assuming that's not the case, you have no worry regarding return; i.e., you know the end result when you make the purchase. And controlling the maturity is no problem since they can be purchased with a due date from a few months to thirty years. Zeros are a peace-of-mind investment because you don't have to reinvest the interest; that's built into the bond.

Note: You must pay taxes on the unpaid interest the bond earns every year, which is why I only recommend them for tax-deferred accounts like your IRA or 401K.

7. BUY COLLATERAL MORTGAGE OBLIGATIONS. CMOs are mortgage bond obligations backed by real estate

mortgage securities, like the Government National Mortgage Association. They can be purchased through a broker for a minimum of $1,000.00. Their rates are generally a percentage point or so higher than Treasury issues with a like term.

It's best to consider CMOs in a long-term light.

8. REAL ESTATE. There are many areas of the country that are in a recession, which offers those with long-term money outstanding real estate opportunities. Investment property can be bought on the cheap. In many cases, through owner financing, with no money down. And REOs are everywhere.

Rental property may be the best investment for small investors. If you buy right, and have a positive rental/net cash flow, there is money to be made, even in depressed areas.

Another possibility: you can purchase an option to buy many substantial properties for as little as $500.00 per year. Granted there's risk, but if you option the right property and find a buyer for an amount exceeding your option price, your returns can be astronomical.

For those who don't feel comfortable owning investment real estate, there are real estate investment trusts (REITs). While many have fallen on hard times, there are some worth considering. Check with your broker for details.

9. GOVERNMENT BONDS. Government notes and bonds can be purchased directly from the Treasury, which saves you the fees associated with many other investments.

Additionally, depending on your state's income tax rate, you can save substantial sums because their interest is often exempt from state tax. And if interest rates fall, bonds can be sold at a profit prior to maturity. You can purchase most issues with as little as $1,000.00.

10. JUNK BONDS. This may surprise you, but junk bonds are worth looking at. Why? Because, after the shake-out they've experienced, there's not much left that can go wrong. Their prices have been drastically cut to reflect their poor performance. The resulting bottomline is you're buying

a severely discounted investment. If you do your homework, the risk on junk bonds can be acceptable.

Of course, notwithstanding the above, I still urge caution.

I hope you'll consider my recommendations. While they are important, they are not the core of the message. The principle of maximizing your returns, regardless of the amount you have to invest, is far more important than any specific counsel. You shouldn't overlook any investment opportunity, even those you previously passed up because you thought they were beyond your means.

Remember, most rich people didn't start out that way. And, while they may have used varying methods to acquire their wealth, they all have one thing in common: they know the results of investing mirror the financial education and intelligence of the investor. If you're an investor with limited resources and limited thinking you're destined to, at best, retain your financial status quo. On the other hand, if you're an investor with limited resources and a financial education, you're almost assured of wealth.

MUTUAL FUNDS

Mutual funds offer so many advantages that they demand attention and consideration from every investor. That's true in the best of times, and even more so now that numerous aspects of the economy force one to consider the possibility of a quasi-depression. Banks are in trouble, the stock market is overvalued, inflation is creeping back, the prime rate is on the way up, increases in our personal taxes are in the works, the FSLIC is bankrupt, and so on. We are on a roller coaster ride that may cost many of the uninformed more than they are willing to spend. The bill for the economic policy failures of government is always paid by the middle-class, and this time will be no exception.

Yet, even in the worst of times there is money to be made. Not that you have any choice. Investing is not open to discussion. No matter what your financial station in life, you have to invest to cement the present and plan for the future. If not, you will be running backward. That's true if your net worth is ten thousand or one hundred million dollars.

So we are presented with a problem. We have to invest and yet the market, as everyone knows, is not a level playing field. Even if that weren't the case, you have to realize the market is no place for amateurs because investing is a full-time job, or should be. There are investment techniques which will give you direction in your investment choices. But, even if you are successful in investment choice, there may be after-the-fact problems, not of your making, that cause your success to become a loss. The bottomline? If you're good, real good, you'll be wrong a good deal of the time. Don't let that bother you, as most so-called experts are too. Experts live off their few successes and forget their numerous failures. Unfortunately, most of us can't afford to play that game. We have to beat the odds.

Let's get to mutual funds specifically. First of all, they offer the chance to play the market, exercise your investment choice (for instance, growth funds, precious metals funds, high tech funds, medical funds, etc.), and still have the security of employing an expert who has something to lose. That's a much different relationship than a straight broker association. Funds allow you to use your common sense and move your money as changes in the economy dictate. But, more importantly, mutual funds offer the following:

1. LOW RISK. Mutual funds are highly regulated. They provide safety within the confines of an investment; i.e., a health service mutual fund may get out of company "X" because the company has problems. If you were invested in that stock, as opposed to a fund that has a portion of its money in the company, you would more than likely lose money, whereas a fund will cushion or negate the reversal. Risk is further decreased because fund managers don't last long with bad results, which means they have a vested interest in results, not just sales commissions.

2. DIVERSIFICATION. This is especially helpful to the smaller investor. A fund can give you access to stocks that by yourself you might not be able to afford. Currently, a fund cannot have more than 5% of its assets in any one company, which forces diversification and added safety.

3. LOW OR NO COST. Mutual fund shares have the commission included in the shares, and/or these shares may actually have no fee whatsoever. They also allow for fractional shares, which, again for the smaller investor, is important. Try and avoid funds with substantial fees.

4. LIQUIDITY. They are almost as liquid as cash. Certainly, they are more liquid than a bank time certificate of deposit and, in fact, can be turned around faster than many stock transactions.

5. LOW MINIMUMS. They allow entry for as little as $100.00. That's a compelling reason to consider funds, as how often can you get these kinds of returns with so little to start?

6. PROFESSIONAL MANAGEMENT. As mentioned earlier, you have to be a professional or employ one. A mutual fund relationship provides necessary financial expertise.

7. FLEXIBILITY. Most funds have a parallel money market account for their customers. Meaning, as circumstances dictate a return to a cash position, all you have to do is make a phone call (usually toll-free), and transfer what you think prudent. Mutual funds money market interest rates are very competitive, and usually exceed what the financial institution industry is offering.

8. PRODUCES PROFITS IN BULL OR BEAR MARKETS. Most mutual fund companies have a number of different funds that offer varying specialties. That means you can shift from yesterday's hot stock(s) to what's hot now.

And do mutual funds compare favorably with other market investments? Historically, as an industry, they beat all comers. Even with a safety factor that the market doesn't offer, mutual funds, under most market conditions, will substantially eclipse what you might be able to garner on your own.

There are hundreds of funds you should consider. To review them, look in a newsstand variety financial publication that offers monthly listings. Find the ones that interest you and call for their prospectus. You should be looking for a long-term track record. Don't be impressed with short-term successes, as even a blind dog turns up a bone once in awhile.

Mutual funds are a unique investment tool. Their returns are more than competitive, with a fraction of the risk offered by most investment vehicles. They are more flexible, diversified and liquid, too. And they cost little or nothing to purchase. They should be a portion of your portfolio.

I've always been pleased with the results of mutual fund investments. Now, more than ever, I see their potential in a market that could be in turmoil rather quickly. Of course, the ultimate responsibility rests with you. Just because you invest in mutual funds doesn't mean you won't be hurt if the market corrects and/or revalues itself. At that point you have to be in the right mutual fund, which, if you oversee your investment, is easily accomplished.

DISCOUNT PROFITEERING

For those who have, or know how to get, available cash
of a moderate to sizable sum, there is a virtually unknown
wealth maker that needs to be explored — I call it discount
profiteering. This plan works on the principle that some
people, for whatever reason, are willing to take less cash
now than more later.

We are going to review this procedure, using real estate
as an example, but the outline is applicable to other financial transactions, as people's need for immediate cash is the
same whether they own a home, a business, or other asset.
Discount profiteering works in almost all transactions that
involve long-term financing. While having some reservations
about real estate investing for the average family, I use it as
an illustration because it, perhaps more than others, makes
the mechanics clear. More importantly, as you will soon see,
when discount profiteering, the investor, in this example,
will not be investing in real estate, he will be investing in
real estate financing, which is a different subject.

One of the key ingredients of discount profiteering is the
recent phenomenon of owner financing. This may apply to a
business purchase, commercial property, or investment
property, but most often it's used for home mortgages.
Owner financing has become exceptionally popular during
times when the home market softens, and/or the cost of
home financing is prohibitive. Even in the best of times it's
hard to sell a home at today's inflated prices, as it's almost
impossible for many couples to make the monthly mortgage
payments required to amortize the loan. Put this scenario
together and you have an average, nothing special, house
costing $100,000.00 or more. With a 30% downpayment re-
quirement, the purchaser must have $30,000.00 in cash, and
will be making payments of almost $700.00 per month, plus
an unknown amount for taxes and insurance. These are not
the ideal circumstances in which to sell property. Hence,
owner financing, which takes the form of a first or second
mortgage.

A seller offers to become a mortgage holder for a number of reasons. First, in many instances, it may be the difference between selling or not selling the home. It also expands the potential market for the property; i.e., with the right financing package, almost everyone becomes a potential buyer. Additionally, assuming the seller has no immediate requirement for the money represented by the mortgage, they start earning a reliable monthly income via the buyer's mortgage payments. More importantly, seller financing usually guarantees you, the seller, your asking price. Plus, in effect, it removes all negotiation rights from the buyer. Plus, you can often — since you're "offering" so much more than an identical house for sale right down the street — ask more for the property.

The flip side of the deal, the buyer's interests, assuming they can afford the payment(s), are also positive. Since, without it they wouldn't be able to buy the home.

Using our $100,000.00 example loan, let's assume the seller offers to finance the downpayment of $30,000.00 because the buyer, while creditworthy, doesn't have enough for the downpayment. The first mortgage will be garnered from a financial institution. The deal looks like this:

1. The seller receives their full asking price.

2. The seller is paid $70,000.00 in cash from the mortgage closing.

3. The seller takes back a second mortgage of $30,000.00 leading to twenty years (an arbitrary term) of monthly payments/income.

4. The buyer receives the property they desire.

5. The buyer buys-in at $0.00 instead of the $30,000.00 it would have taken using traditional means.

This deal could have taken many forms. For example, maybe the buyer had $10,000.00 down, which would then have only required a second mortgage of $20,000.00. These deals are negotiable. I used a simple first and second mort-gage to make the principle easy to understand.

To carry our example further, we have to apply an interest rate to the twenty year second mortgage. I'm using 12%. Payments are $330.33. Meaning the second mortgage note has a total value of $79,279.20 ($330.33 x 12 months x 20 years). We, for obvious reasons, are not concerned with the first mortgage.

As quite often happens, the financial needs of those in long-term financial relationships change. It is this occurrence that allows the prepared investor to make returns the likes of which they may have never seen.

A side, but important note: you can advertise for such properties by stating that you buy discounted mortgages for cash. It's amazing the number of responses such ads generate.

Continuing our example: Let's say the seller, now second mortgage holder, has decided he needs to turn the mortgage into cash at the five year mark. He sees the ad. At the end of five years the second mortgage has a principal balance of $27,522.96. The holder has a choice of doing nothing, thereby continuing to earn $330.33 a month for the next fifteen years, or taking an offer to buy the mortgage for $20,000.00. Why would he take such an offer? He needs cash, it's that simple. (Note: I, in an attempt to offer a conservative example, have used what I consider a small discount. In actual practice a persuasive investor would be successful in buying the second mortgage for less.)

Assuming our example seller agrees to the offer, where does the investor stand? Three things can happen:

1. The buyer can continue to make his payments for the next fifteen years.

2. The buyer can default.

3. The buyer can sell the property prior to the loan coming to term.

Let's review the ramifications of each possibility:

1. Since the starting point of the participation in the loan is the five year mark, there are only fifteen years left — the total to be repaid during that time is $59,459.40 ($330.33 x 12 months x 15 years). This amortization is calculated on the original term of twenty years at $30,000.00. But, our investor only has $20,000.00 invested. That differential means his yearly return jumps to 18.6%, or 6.6 percentage points above the face value of the note, as his investment is $7,522.96 less while his dollar return remains constant. Again, this is a conservative example. Imagine the return if he negotiated a $10,000.00 discount.

Regardless, even our example should get your attention. After all, when's the last time you locked-in almost 19% on such a secured investment?

2. This, by far, is the least likely occurrence. As the investor holds a second mortgage, he has to buy-out the first mortgage holder to secure his position. For this I recommend a short-term note, possibly from the bank holding the first mortgage. They aren't in the real estate business and probably will welcome the chance to get out of a possible foreclosure situation. Consequently, they, in most instances, will exchange a loan default, and the associated inconvenience, for the investor's credit rating, which I assume is excellent.

Using a yearly inflation factor of 5%, this property will have appreciated $25,000.00 during the five years. We now have an asset worth $125,000.00. Against the property there's a remaining first mortgage balance of $68,364.16, a second mortgage worth $27,522.96, for a total of $95,887.12. That leaves the investor with an equity position of $29,112.88 ($125,000.00 - $95,887.12).

With that amount of leverage, it is inconceivable that the home couldn't be sold immediately.

This assumes a voluntary return of collateral. However, even if a foreclosure is required, the investor is secured. Of course, the return to the investor depends on when the default occurs. If, in our example, it happened in the first year it would have been 37.6%.

3. This is the most likely scenario, as the average home is sold every five years.

Assume this home is sold five years after the purchase of the second mortgage. The investor spent $20,000.00. During the five years he held the note, he collected $19,819.80 ($330.33 x 12 months x 5 years). The remaining principal balance of the second mortgage is $23,010.00, which he will be paid at the closing of the sale. The difference between his original investment and the close-out is $3,010.00 ($23,010.00 - $20,000.00), which should be added to his payments to arrive at a total of $22,829.80 ($19,819.80 + $3,010.00). He invested $20,000.00 for five years and was paid $22,829.80 — that's a yearly return of 22.8%%.

As an investment vehicle, this has few limitations. It's just a matter of how much you win. Returns of 30 and 40 percent are not uncommon.

As I mentioned earlier, this plan has other applications. For instance, thousands of businesses are financed by the former owner, in part or total. Maybe the mortgage holder is in poor health, needs to move, or is deceased and the family wants a lump sum payment to close out the estate. There are a multitude of reasons why people are receptive to selling an earning asset at a discount. Aggressive investors understand and are prepared to profit from this little known fact of financial life.

Creative financing should make you realize that discount profiteering can be applied using other people's money, no money down techniques, and options, so even if you don't have cash laying around, you can still play the game. Further, you'll find that discounting works regardless of economic conditions.

Discount profiteering offers the unusual potential of safety and huge profit. That's an investment combination which deserves your attention.

HOW TO SAVE UP TO $500,000.00 OR MORE
AT NO COST TO YOU

Is it really possible to save up to $500,000.00 or more at no cost? Amazingly, yes.

Not surprisingly, to achieve this important financial accomplishment, you must deviate from traditional thinking. The process involves your home mortgage.

For most of us, the one time we are forced to deal with our bank or savings and loan association is when we buy a home. Since few of us can afford to pay cash, you are looking at a long-term mortgage loan commitment. Before getting to the mortgage and its amortization, you have to have a basic understanding of how a mortgage works. Mortgages are usually the largest debt your family will incur, and that fact alone should get your attention. It is probably the largest monthly expense in the family budget, but most people never understand what a home actually costs. If they paid $100,000.00 for the house they think that was their cost. Wrong. The cost of the house is what you pay in total, and that includes your mortgage repayment.

When the bank offers a loan rate and quotes the monthly payment, the family simply decides whether or not they can afford that expense. If the answer is yes, they go ahead. Very seldom do they calculate the total to be repaid. The financial institution would rather that you never do. It might cause you to question the loan.

It is a good rule of thumb that, for every dollar of mortgage money you borrow, you will pay back, depending on the interest rate, three to four and a half dollars. Consequently, if you borrow $100,000.00, you are going to pay back $300,000.00 to $450,000.00. More than likely, when you signed your mortgage agreement, the lender never made that information terribly obvious. Typically, the bank's mortgage documentation will tell you what your monthly payment is, when it's due, the Annual Percentage Rate (APR), the closing costs, the loan's term, etc., but they seldom make it easy for you to determine how much you will ultimately repay. Borrowing $100,000.00 is one thing, owing $300,000.00 to $450,000.00 is another. Look at your house. Is it really worth that much?

Determining your total mortgage obligation is easy: multiply your monthly payment times 12 (months in the year). Multiply the answer times your loan's term, for example, 29 or 30 years.

When you are talking about a debt as large as your mortgage, it behooves you to try and lower your interest rate, but that's another subject. Right now I simply want to make you aware of the important concept: loan rates are negotiable. An aggressive loan customer can take advantage of this little known fact. Calculate how much money you will borrow in your lifetime and factor in even a small one percentage point reduction in costs. You will be stunned at the savings that can be realized. You must be willing to negotiate and haggle in order to retain as much of your earnings as possible. I estimate that, through simple rate negotiations you can, at a minimum, save as much as $50,000.00 over the course of your financial lifetime. And that figure doesn't take into account the additional money you could make by investing those savings.

Remember, any loan interest rate reduction is worth fighting for. Don't settle for less than a fair deal. Banks make good loan customers like yourself pay more than they should so they can offset their losses with their bad loan customers. You can't afford to pay for the bank's lending mistakes. (NOTE: From this point forward we are going to use as an example a mortgage loan of $150,000.00 at 12% for thirty years. The loan has monthly payments of $1,542.92 for a total repayment cost of $555,451.20.)

The first thing you must do is realize that if you follow the bank's loan amortization schedule (monthly payment timetable) there is nothing I, or anyone else, can do to reduce the true net cost of your home. The reason is obvious when you realize that mortgage payments are recalculated every month on a declining balance. Which means, it will be many years before you even start denting the principal. For example, in our sample loan the first payment is broken down as follows:

Total payment $1,542.92
Interest   1,500.00
Principal reduction   42.92

The first month's principal reduction is only 2.78% of the payment. You can see how, with this schedule, you will be paying the bank back virtually forever, which is exactly what the bank wants.

How do we turn this around? The answer is, you must add an additional principal payment with each monthly payment. For our example, I will use an added $100.00 per month. When you make an added monthly payment, the entire amount is subtracted from the loan's principal. When you make the bank's first scheduled payment of $1,542.92 your loan is only reduced $42.92, but when you add just $100.00 more, you reduce the principal by double that amount.

What effect does this have on your loan? The startling answer in this example is that, by making this small (6.48%) additional payment, you will repay your thirty year loan in just twenty years. You reduced your obligation by ten years of $185,150.40 ($1,542.92 x 12 months x 10 years). And all it cost you was $24,000.00 ($100.00 x 12 months x 20 years). Let's look at the net cost of the home so far:

Payments to bank $370,300.80
$100.00 additional payments $24,000.00
Total $394,300.80

Granted, that's still a lot of money, but we have gone a long way towards recovering your scheduled mortgage payments. Look at the savings:

Bank amortization cost $555,451.20
New total cost $394,300.80
Total savings $161,150.40

This should make clear that you should never accept the bank's way of doing business. It's just too costly. You must use nontraditional alternatives.

We have made substantial progress but we haven't reached our unstated goal of completely recovering the mortgage expense. The accelerated loan repayment was just the first step in our system. As it stands, we have saved 29% of what the example loan would have cost. Only 71% to go.

The next step is using the saving of time accumulated by the first step. If you were willing to pay the bank the last ten years, you should be willing to pay yourself instead. In this case, you would continue to make your monthly payments of $1,542.92, but they would be made to your saving or investment program. What would your accumulated investment be worth with payments of $1,542.92 invested in a plan that returned 10% (you should be able to average this rate or better) over the last ten years of what is now your paid-off mortgage? The answer is an amazing $316,059.41.

Of course, if you make these payments to yourself, you still have an expenditure and that must be recalculated into your net cost. That is to say, the comparison must again be on the amount you actually paid. It doesn't matter who the money went to. Let's review where we are:

Paid by customer (to bank and self) $555,451.20

Balance of savings plan after nine years $316,059.41

Unrecovered mortgage expense $239,391.79

We aren't doing too badly. By ignoring the bank's amortization schedule and adding as little as $100.00 per month to your payment you saved $161,150.40, or ten years worth of expense minus the added monthly payments. Then by using the ten years to your advantage and making what was a liability into an asset, your savings jumped to a whopping $316,059.41. We have now saved 56.9% of the real cost of your home.

The next and final step actually must be the first step you have to take in order to recover the entire cost of your scheduled mortgage payments. It's imperative when you buy a home that you dissect the entire transaction. That is, the total mortgage repayment, the added payments you will make, and what the savings balance will be at the end of the thirty years. You should have this information available for your own education and, more importantly, to determine the final piece of the puzzle. In my example, you would still have an unrecovered mortgage expense of $239,391.79. To recoup that amount, you are going to buy a Grade A Municipal Bond from a local security house. This purchase must be made at the time you sign your mortgage, and it should have the same term as your mortgage. In our example, we are using a percentage of 6.5% to buy the bond. This rate changes daily and could be higher or lower, but that won't adversely affect the end result. In this case, the bond would cost $15,560.47 (239,391.79 x .065; you should refactor this into your equation so that the cost of the bond is recovered). At the end of thirty years you will receive $239,391.79 in cash and it all will be free of federal income taxes. It is assumed you can afford to pay cash for the bond and, if that's the case, you are finished.

Those who are not able to afford the bond purchase can borrow additional money in their mortgage. Enough to buy the bond. Of course, the added amount will have to be recalculated in your program, but it won't change the bottomline which is this: at the end of the term of your loan you will have your home free and clear and all of your scheduled mortgage payments in the bank in your name.

This system is, by necessity, flexible. There are many variables to consider. For example: you may wish to borrow money for the bond on a short term note of your own choosing, as opposed to adding the cost to your mortgage. Maybe you make additional monthly payments of only $50.00 or as much as $200.00. Perhaps your savings plan returns as little as 8%, or maybe as much as 13%. There are no parameters to the system, which is to your advantage. Notwithstanding particulars, one thing cannot be denied — you are either going to pay your mortgage holder or pay yourself. The choice seems obvious. Their way, at the end of thirty years, you will have your home free and clear. My way, at the end of 30 years, you'll have your home free and clear, plus, using this example, a savings plan and municipal bond totaling $555,451.20. And the beauty is, it didn't cost you a penny more than you were willing to pay for the house alone.

BUYING REOS

Historically, foreclosed real estate properties were poorly maintained, rundown, located in bad neighborhoods, and probably not the kind of single family residence you'd want to live in or buy for rental income. Nor would you want to make one an investment through resale. But times have changed.

REO stands for "real estate owned by lender", and in today's market most financial institutions have their share. Then there are the numerous government agencies which have foreclosure properties. The VA, Federal Housing Administration, the Federal National Mortgage Corporation are a few examples. Credit unions also have REOs. The point is, the market in REOs is expanding. Expanding rapidly. That means opportunities for those who are prepared and understand how to use institutional misfortune for personal gain.

The reason for this expanded market is simple. Many homes are overpriced to start with, which means they are overfinanced. Others were builder-subsidized to allow the buyer entry to property actually beyond their ability to repay. Then there is the Adjustable Rate Mortgage (ARM). Many people who started off being able to afford their home have found, through upward rate adjustments, that the home is now out of their affordable monthly budget range. This particular problem is just going to get worse. There is the very real possibility that ARM's will be the cause of record foreclosures in the very near future. If inflation does what I think it will do, which means the prime rate will be affected, housing costs could increase 50% for the home you presently own. The result? More foreclosures. I should also mention geography here. Many sections of the country, like Texas and the Northeast, are depressed. That means more foreclosures. Unfortunately, I believe this market has barely started.

The good news is that, because of unusual and new circumstances, some of these foreclosed houses are virtually brand new. And I'm not just talking about low cost housing. Many are middle to upper class housing. That was never true before.

1. WHERE TO LOOK. Practically every city has properties for auction. Finding them is as easy as reading the monthly or weekly newspaper listing from the government agency indicating their current REO properties that will be up for auction. Property is available for inspection prior to the sale. Participants have to arrive with cash or a certified check to bid — this requirement varies by agency.

There is an immediate cash downpayment requirement should your bid be accepted. However, in most cases, if you can't pay the remaining balance, or acquire financing before their time limitations, you lose your monies already paid. This indicates you should do your homework before the fact. Later may be too late.

2. THE BEST MARKET. I have reservations about government REOs. They are usually the worst of the lot.

The real market is financial institutions. They presently have thousands of single family homes that are in foreclosure. And they are normally good property. Why? Because, even though the former owners defaulted, they once qualified for a standard mortgage. That means they probably had a 20 to 30% downpayment. Consequently, they probably made repairs, etc., to protect their equity. Bank REOs also tend to be in better neighborhoods, because even though they would deny this, banks still practice red-lining. Also, banks will upkeep the home as long as they own it, so, unlike government REOs, they usually are in better repair.

The best part of dealing with a financial institution is that you are not bidding against anyone. Unlike the government, banks don't advertise their problems. Only if you ask do you get to play the game. There is no auction. No government requirements. No red tape. It's you against them in a straight sale. Clearly that's to your advantage.

Finding bank REOs is as easy as stopping into your local banks and asking to see the officer in charge of foreclosed single-residence properties. If you're looking for rental properties, ask for them directly.

Tell the bank you are interested in purchasing properties in such and such a range, in such and such an area, and ask what they have available. Bank officers, under these circumstances, are usually quite helpful. They need to unload their REOs as soon as possible. For a change, they need you more than you need them, so don't seem too anxious. Realize that the prices they will quote are negotiable. Obviously they want to get as much as they can, but they won't lose a sale if you're close to their requirements. Which, by the way, may be well below the market value of the property.

Another important aspect of bank REO buying is that the bank may be more than willing to help you finance the purchase. Their requirements for this kind of credit are far below what they would ask if you just walked in off the street asking for standard mortgage consideration on a home not presently in their delinquent/foreclosed home portfolio. Negotiation is the key to making this a big winner. Don't be afraid to ask for substantial, even unusual, concessions. REOs are a special breed.

3. CAUTIONS. If you're buying from a government agency, you should employ a professional appraiser. You need someone to inspect the property for physical defects, as many REOs have structural problems that can get very costly. Also, because of possible neighborhood problems, don't just look at the price. If you don't want to live in a neighborhood, chances are not many others will either. In other words, an expensive house in a declining neighborhood is worthless. That price that looked so good at the auction may be twice what you can sell it for, so be careful.

Financial institution REOs require common sense, at least as much as you would use buying a home in the normal sense. It wouldn't hurt to spend a couple of hundred extra dollars to have an appraiser confirm your opinion of the property's worth. Your odds of getting hurt are much less with a bank than with the government, but don't be lulled into a false sense of security.

Regardless of where you purchase a REO, you should have a lawyer review all your documentation. You know how much I dislike using lawyers, but in this case it's required. Why? Because foreclosure properties oftentimes have title problems. A mistake here can cost you all your profit and more. Hire a lawyer for the closing.

REOs are a growing market. One that you should be considering either for housing or investment. For anyone willing to spend a little time and effort, the gains can be quite amazing. Statistically, you'll average a savings of approximately 15% from government REOs. Bank savings approximate 20%, although savings of 40% are not unheard of. Frankly, because I believe the market will grow beyond what most anticipate, the savings percentages should start going up. Each and every day, banks and the government add to their REO stockpile. That means the cost to the wise consumer or investor will start going down proportionately. Now is the time to explore the market. The only real mistake you can make is ignoring this opportunity.

HOW TO PREVENT PROBLEMS
WITH YOUR BROKER

Believe it or not, even after the Crash of '87 and the numerous associated disputes between investors and their brokers, the actual number of disputes has not abated. In short, little was learned from the Crash. The brokers are still in a business-as-usual mode, and investors haven't become more aggressive in protecting their rights. In fact, just the opposite has occurred. Brokers are trying to find ways to protect themselves even further from accountability, at a time when they should be more responsible. Perhaps they cannot be blamed entirely, as the lack of concern and action from investors plays a large part in the industry's audacity.

Regardless, based on history and current events, one thing is sure — you'd better know how to protect your market assets. Here are three important recommendations:

1. BE WARY OF ARBITRATION CLAUSES. Many brokerage agreements have a arbitration clause that, in effect, removes your right to sue your broker, even if they have broken a criminal law. Regardless of the severity of the offense, you cannot sue — you must go to arbitration.

That's bad enough, but if you look closely, you'll find that, in almost all instances, you have to use an industry arbitration board to resolve your complaint. Simply stated, your case will be decided by other brokers and/or market insiders. Any time an industry polices itself, the public's rights are abridged. As you might guess, the securities industry, in all but the most blatant cases, sticks together to protect the brotherhood.

Regardless of your feelings on the subject of broker errors or illegalities, giving away your right to sue is not prudent. Find a brokerage house that doesn't require such a waiver.

For those of you who already signed such an agreement, send your broker a certified letter, return receipt requested, stating that you are terminating the arbitration clause.

Make clear that they are not to transact any additional business in your account unless they accept the change. If they process transactions after receipt of the letter, you have a course of action if there is a problem. If they decide they only want your account under their inequitable terms, it's better that you find another broker, so don't be disappointed by a negative response.

Retaining your right to sue, more than anything, will help protect your market investments.

2. RETAIN HANDS-ON CONTROL OF YOUR AC-COUNT. Too many investors open their account and leave the rest up to their broker. That's an error. Make it unmistakable to your broker that you want to be informed of events that may have an impact on your account. Most brokers only call with a sales pitch or bad news. A good broker calls with relevant news that will allow you to better manage your investments.

Of course, to retain control of your account, you have to spend time and effort keeping current with the market and your stocks. If your broker is your sole source of reference you're in trouble. Remember, brokers get paid to sell. They don't believe they're there to manage your assets, unless such management culminates in additional sales. Unfortunately, their goals are not consistent with your objectives. That's why you have to make the point that you're in control.

3. KEEP YOUR INVESTMENTS SIMPLE. It may be nice to have an extensive portfolio, and certainly diversification is necessary, but the fact is, for most investors, a simple account is the best account.

The market is complicated and, unless you are a legitimate expert, you shouldn't be considering naked options, margin transactions, etc. Your broker, for his own purposes, may want you in such complicated transactions, but they are not advisable. Quite the contrary. Most investors should have a standard stock portfolio, mutual funds, and a cash account. The more complex, the greater the risk.

To expand on this point, I strongly suggest not becoming involved in a discretionary account. Most people are not aware that a brokerage house has a right to call for immediate settlement on their margin calls. With the knowledge the Crash of '87 should have brought, you can see why such a call during a market crisis could be catastrophic. A broker may, at his sole discretion, close out your position(s) if he believes he, or his house, might be vulnerable. The bottomline? Brokers will protect their assets by damaging yours. Common sense alone dictates simplicity.

Many investors have lowered the guard they had raised immediately after the Crash. That's a mistake, because the same mechanics that exacerbated the Crash are still being used today. The S.E.C. and Congress have done little to protect the average investor, even though they promised to do so immediately following Black Monday.

Because of their irresponsibility, a Crash could happen again. Which means a flood of investor/broker disputes will likely reoccur. Except this time the investor will be to blame. You have been warned; i.e., if your account relationship with your brokerage house is still the same, or was changed for the worse since the Crash, what happens from here on is your fault.

Preventive maintenance is not optional, it's compulsory.

FINANCIAL PLANNERS

The vast majority of financial planners are nothing more than salesmen. They, like many stockbrokers, recommend what's good for themselves, as opposed to what's good for their clients. Worse yet, unlike your broker, financial planners are not regulated in any substantive manner.

As the concept of financial planners became acceptable in the marketplace, everyone started calling themselves a financial planner when, in fact, they had no education or experience in the field. For example, suddenly, insurance salesmen became financial planners. Why? Because it allowed them to represent their sales pitch as investment advice. It became more palatable to the client. Their obvious conflict of interest was hidden from view. Sales increased. The investors? You guessed it, they lost — as usual. A good rule of thumb when dealing with a financial planner is, IF HE'S SELLING ANYTHING OTHER THAN ADVICE DON'T DO BUSINESS WITH HIM.

This is not to say you shouldn't use a financial planner. Quite the contrary. A reputable planner may be able, for a reasonable cost, to design a long term plan for your finances that will be exceptionally profitable and meet your needs and expectations.

Everyone should consider a financial planner. The problem is finding a good one, as the industry is loaded with frauds, con-artists, and disguised salesmen. The truth is, there are far more bad financial planners than good ones. Asking your prospective financial planner the following questions will help you locate the one right for you:

1. WHAT IS YOUR FORMAL EDUCATION IN THE FINANCIAL PLANNING FIELD? If he doesn't have any that you can verify, you'd best steer clear. Remember, most financial planners got that title by giving it to themselves.

2. WHAT IS YOUR FINANCIAL PLANNING EXPERIENCE? If he doesn't have a proven, extensive track record,

keep looking. You cannot afford to have him learning the ropes with your money.

3. MAY I HAVE A LIST OF YOUR CLIENTS THAT I CAN CONTACT? If he doesn't have any, or he invokes confidentiality, he is not a professional of any standing.

4. MAY I HAVE A LIST OF YOUR ATTORNEY, CPA, AND BANKER? You need to talk to these people to ascertain the professional status of your potential planner.

Oftentimes, even if you like the planner, after talking to his attorney, CPA, or banker, you will find out a number of facts and figures that may force you to alter your opinion. This simple background check is mandatory.

5. ARE YOU LICENSED BY THE STATE? In most states a financial planner needs to be licensed if he or she charges commissions. A planner not complying with this simple legal requirement shouldn't be trusted with your money.

However, as I don't recommend planners for *anything* other than financial plan formulation, the commission aspect is actually moot.

6. MAY I HAVE A COPY OF A RECENT PLAN? It pays to see a copy of a planner's work. He can retain the confidentiality of the other client by blacking out any names in the report, so don't accept confidentiality as a reason for denying your request.

When you see a finished plan, you will have a good idea of the planner's professional competence. (If it's a computer printed plan watch out — see Question #7.)

7. HOW DO YOU ARRIVE AT A PLAN? If a planner uses a computer program, say thank you and goodbye. A financial plan must be tailored to be effective. There are a number of computer programs that prepare plans by simply putting in a few raw numbers. The plans look good, but are worthless. Your plan deserves individual thought and consideration.

8. WHO WILL PREPARE MY PLAN? If someone on the planner's staff will prepare the plan, ask to see and talk to

that person. Too often you have interviews with one person only to have another, completely unfamiliar with your situation, actually do the work. This doesn't work for all the obvious reasons.

9. MAY I SEE YOUR TAX RETURNS FOR THE LAST THREE YEARS? Many of you may be surprised at this question, but, while I know it may cause difficulty in your relationship with your prospective planner, it is required.

The planner will, out of necessity, ask to see your tax returns. They need to see where you have been, and where you are, before they can assist you in determining where you're going. In a trusting financial relationship you will see the need for providing this information. Conversely, if you are going to trust this individual with a portion of your financial future, wouldn't you like to know if he can handle his own finances? If he and his firm are not financially successful, why should you trust him with your finances? The answer is, you shouldn't.

10. WHAT ARE YOUR PROFESSIONAL CREDENTIALS? The best credential is certification as a Certified Financial Planner. This doesn't mean he is capable, but it's a start.

If you're told that the planner is a member of the International Association of Financial Planning (IAFP), don't be too impressed. Anyone with an interest in the subject can join. On the other hand, if he is a member of the IAFP's Registry, he has passed a test and review that indicates a minimum of expertise.

He should also be a member of the National Association of Personal Financial Advisors.

11. CHECKING ON CREDENTIALS. The financial planning industry is new and virtually devoid of regulation, but the following is available:

The Institute of Certified Financial Planners
2 Denver Highlands
10065 E. Harvard Ave., Suite 320

Denver, CO 80231
Phone: 303-751-7600

International Association for Financial Planning
2 Concourse Parkway, Suite 800
Atlanta, GA 30328
Phone: 404-395-1605

While I am not satisfied with the present professional clearing houses for financial planners, you still must avail yourself of what little information exists. Run a check through these associations.

The concept of using a financial planner makes sense even if you receive nothing more than additional independent guidance that assists you in formulating your own plan. If you need a complete plan, that's fine too. In either case, you must protect yourself from those in the market who call themselves financial planners when, in fact, they are nothing of the kind.

The industry is overloaded with glorified salesmen and cheats, so use an overdose of caution. That's the bad news. The good news is, if you can find a good one, one you can trust, a financial planner and the plan he engineers may be the best investment you ever make.

YOUR HOME

BUYING A HOME

With the cost of housing in most areas now averaging well over $100,000.00, it has become more apparent than ever that a home is a big investment. For most families, it is the biggest investment they'll ever make. Unfortunately, most of them will never realize that fact.

Not only is the cost of a home substantial, the repayment of the mortgage is staggering. For example, a standard $100,000.00 mortgage at 13% for 30 years will cost you $398,232.00. That's a rather large sum to pay for a standard home, but that's the way a mortgage works. But, this section is more concerned with the actual home purchase than its financing.

Most home buyers have no idea of what they are doing in a technical sense. They buy what they like. Very seldom is much thought given to the home as an investment. If that were the case, buyers wouldn't ignore the structure, building quality, etc., which they do almost universally.

The very same people who wouldn't consider buying a used car without a mechanic inspecting the vehicle, buy a home without one-tenth the caution. What's the end result? Repairs, Costs. Overpayment on the home's real worth. Disappointment. Future repair costs. Difficulty in selling the property at a later date. Many negatives accrue when you don't use caution in purchasing a home. Failure on this important consideration will cost you money. In some cases large sums.

There are ways to insure that doesn't happen to you:

1. HIRE AN ENGINEER, CONTRACTOR, OR HOUSING EXPERT TO INSPECT THE PROPERTY. The cost should be around $150.00. In some areas, home inspection contractors advertise in the phone book. Since there is some

expense here, you only want to employ an inspector when you're very serious about a property. This will be money well spent.

Since you don't want to run up your costs, you should have some ability to inspect a home by yourself before you call an inspector. The following tips will help.

2. LOOK IN THE BASEMENT FIRST. That's the foundation of the entire structure, and if there are problems, they often show up here before becoming obvious elsewhere.

Look for water marks on the walls that indicate a flooding problem. Look for cracks other than those that are only of the surface variety. Look for fresh painting, which is oftentimes used to cover up patches.

Check the basement's smell. Odors usually mean water problems and/or sewer seepage.

Look for floor braces put in after construction; these indicate a very big problem.

Check the floor joints. Poke around with a knife. Any soft spots? Bad news if you find any. Look for termites, bugs, carpenter ants, etc. Again, a major problem.

The fuse box should have at least 16 circuits with breakers. If we're talking about an older house, you may be looking at a complete rewiring. Your hired inspector can give you a good cost estimate should you proceed with this house.

Look for any basement floor buckling which is a sure sign that there is a major problem about to happen. The ground or the house is shifting. This happens quite often with foundations that are poured during the winter; i.e., they never settle right. The problem may not show up for years, but it will show up.

Check the water heater. It should be approximately 60 gallons if it's an electric heater. Forty if it's gas. Look for corrosion, damage, obvious problems.

A close-up view of the furnace is required. Look for rust, corrosion. Also, if it's summertime don't forget to have the owner turn on the furnace for you! Many summertime buyers find out later the furnace doesn't work at all, or needs major repairs. This same procedure holds true for air conditioning.

3. TOUR THE OUTSIDE OF THE HOUSE. Inspect it from all angles. See something out of alignment? Trouble is on its way.

If the home has a brick construction, look to see if any bricks are cracking. Are there any breaks in the mortar between the bricks? If so, the home is either shifting or was poorly constructed.

Look at any outside steps. Do they fit flush or are they crooked. If they're concrete, are they cracking, separating from the house, etc? Another problem sign.

If the home is constructed of wood, inspect the windows and door jams. Rotting shows up here first. Also, if the home has been recently painted, exercise great caution. Paint is not only used to spruce up the place, it's used to cover rot.

Aluminum siding is sometimes a plus. But, on many older homes, it, too, is used to cover rot. Use caution. Older homes need to have their siding looked under, because some aluminum siding is put directly over the old wooden siding, as opposed to having the old siding removed first. Siding doesn't stop rot, so in a few years you will be faced with a major repair bill.

If it's possible, get on the roof. See if you see repair spots which indicate you have leakage problems. Check around the chimney and any ventilators. Often you'll find water damage here. If there is a brick chimney, inspect it closely. A chimney problem may go all the way down to the basement in an older home. Here too, a major repair expense at some point.

4. INSPECT THE INSIDE IN DETAIL. Do you hear any creaks when you walk through the rooms? A possible construction and/or foundation problem.

Do the interior doors close effortlessly? If they stick or are too loose, it may be an indication that the home is shifting.

Check the electrical outlets. Are there enough of them?
If not, you have a sizable expense to meet your needs. Elec-
tricians don't work cheap.

Thoroughly check the ceilings for cracks, separations,
etc., which are a sure sign you've got structural problems.
Check the corners of each room. Separations here aren't
open to debate; you have a home that was poorly constructed
or is shifting badly. If possible, check the attic for structural
problems. These are usually obvious because no one bothers
to hide the repairs, as they aren't normally seen. Also, is
there enough insulation for your area? Ask the owner what
the R factor is for the ceiling and walls on the house. In
many older houses, walls have little or no insulation. If
you're buying in the summer, you may not notice that in
winter the walls may actually produce ice. One way to check
is to ask to see the heating bills for the entire year. If the
winter bills are not reasonable, it's an indication the home is
not well insulated. To fix things will cost a bundle!

5. OTHER IMPORTANT TIPS. Check with the neighbors. They will tell you a lot about the house you are thinking of buying as well as a lot about the neighborhood.

Is it an established neighborhood or a recent subdivi-
sion? Remember, much recent construction is done over
landfills or worse. The house is important — so is the land
it's built on. This may take a little detective work on your
part, but do it. Millions of home buyers have suffered financial and health problems because they didn't do their homework on this subject.

Is the home connected to a sewer system? If not, you'd
better check the septic field or whatever they're using. This
can be a major headache, not to mention the cost, if things
aren't right.

This should give you a starting point to make your own
inspection prior to hiring an expert. Many of the homes you
look at will be turned down out-of-hand using my guidelines,
which will save you money and time.

I haven't touched on more personal considerations here. For instance, do the schools meet your needs? Is the property near factories that have a pollution problem? How about the traffic around your house? Is it too noisy, dangerous, etc.? Do you have nearby police and fire protection? How about garbage collection? These considerations are not reviewed here because, while they are important, they are not structural in nature. Clearly, however, they shouldn't be ignored.

My concern in this section is that you don't spend considerable monies on a home that has problems you could have avoided. Remember, you're not buying a $100,000.00 home. You're buying a $398,232.00 home! You might as well get your money's worth. Not to mention that structural problems may cost more than repair expense. They may cost you money when you sell the home.

A mistake in buying almost always costs again and again, year after year.

HOW TO SAVE TENS OF THOUSANDS OF DOLLARS ON YOUR MORTGAGE

You should always try to reduce your mortgage expense. These important and profitable tips will save you thousands of dollars before, during, and after you sign your mortgage.

1. KNOW WHAT SIZE MORTGAGE YOU CAN AFFORD. Perhaps the biggest mortgage mistake you can make is overextending yourself. This happens to far too many home buyers. The best way to buy a house is to know what you can afford and not exceed that preset limit. When you remember you will repay three to four and a half dollars for every one you borrow, you can see that a mistake in buying can become a hugh mistake in borrowing.

2. SHOP YOUR MORTGAGE NEEDS. That may sound obvious, but it's not to many. They go to their local bank or the one recommended by the real estate agent. That's a mistake. You should shop your mortgage at as many outlets as possible. Try banks, savings and loans, private money, etc. Shopping may take some time, but with an expense the size of your mortgage, the savings are worth the extra legwork.

3. NEGOTIATE YOUR RATE. Here too, an obvious consideration that many ignore. Some are intimidated by banks, others don't understand the technicalities of a mortgage. They're the ones who don't think a small rate reduction is worth fighting for. They couldn't be more wrong. A one percentage point reduction on a thirty-year one hundred thousand dollar mortgage amounts to a savings of almost $27,000.00. Even half a percentage point is worth time and negotiating effort.

4. GET THE RIGHT TERM FOR YOUR NEEDS. Term can be almost as important as interest rate. A thirty year loan at 15% has a monthly payment of $1,266.80 and a total repayment of $440,846.40. The same loan over twenty years has a monthly payment of $1,316.79, and a total repayment of $316,029.60. The monthly difference is $49.99 or 3.9%.

The total repayment savings is $124,816.80, or 28.31%. The right term can save thousands.

5. FIND A FIXED RATE MORTGAGE. While there are some circumstances where an Adjustable Rate Mortgage (ARM) might be profitable, for most it is not. A fixed rate mortgage gives you stability, which is essential in a mortgage. When rates go up, you are sitting on a gold mine. When they go down, you have the option of remortgaging. With an ARM you might lose your house through no fault of your own. A three percentage point up-tick in your ARM can mean an additional expense of over eighty thousand dollars. You don't get a better house, nor any more money — just more debt.

6. DON'T FALL FOR THE ESCROW SCAM. Demand to pay your taxes and insurance yourself. If that's not possible, ensure that your escrow account receives a market interest rate. Many financial institutions demand an escrow account, but pay no interest. If you agree to that unfair requirement, you are making the bank an interest-free loan every year, throughout the term of your mortgage. You deserve the thousands of dollars your escrow account will earn.

7. LOWER YOUR CLOSING COSTS. In today's market, you can spend thousands of dollars in closing costs before you get the privilege of making what is probably an over-priced mortgage payment. Just like mortgage rates, mortgage closing costs have to be shopped and negotiated. Closing costs are even more critical when you realize that most homes sell every three and a half to five years. You can't afford to pay closing costs based on a thirty year amortization when the loan will probably run one-sixth that time.

8. POINTS VS. RATE. Presently, most mortgage buyers are forced to make a choice. A higher interest rate and lower closing costs, or a lower interest rate and high closing costs. Which is best? It depends on your circumstances. As a general rule of thumb, if you will be in the house for a long time, take the lower rate with higher closing costs. If you will be moving shortly, take the lower costs and higher rate. Take a pencil and figure which is best for your needs. Don't guess.

9. REMORTGAGING. Another general rule of thumb: if interest rates have fallen one percentage point, remortgaging is one method you can't overlook. Find out your new mortgage payment (including your principal and new closing costs) at the lower rate and subtract it from your present monthly cost. Divide your closing costs by the monthly savings and you'll know how long it will take for you to start making money with the remortgaging.

10. EXPLORE ALL YOUR OPTIONS. There are many ways to lower your mortgage expense; review them all. If you can find a way to improve it, do so. For example, if you can afford to make weekly or bi-weekly mortgage payments, you can save a great deal in interest costs. There are other examples. Regardless of the specifics, you cannot afford to overlook any opportunity to lower the real cost of your housing expense.

REDUCING YOUR PROPERTY TAXES

Property taxes are an expense of owning real estate that we've all come to accept. We have come to accept that the local tax assessor has the final word on how much our taxes will be. That's not true.

Many property owners have successfully questioned their real estate taxes and have won. So can you.

To determine if your taxes are excessive, you have to ascertain the property's "fair market value" (the sale price you could reasonably be expected to garner in a normal real estate transaction). Probably the best way to arrive at that value is to have a local real estate broker give you an estimate. Normally a broker will do so for free if you assure them you will use their firm if and when you sell your property.

Once you receive your estimate, you have three possible grounds to challenge your real estate taxes:

1. OVERVALUATION. This occurs when the assessor has made a mistake as to the size and repair of structure(s), and therefore their value. Most "appraisals" done by the assessor are of the "drive-by" variety (that means exactly what it says; i.e., they drive by and put a number to your property's value). This typical appraisal technique takes a minute or two maximum, so you can see there is a great margin for error. This area is perhaps the most useful in our efforts to reduce your real estate taxes.

2. ILLEGALITY. This does not pertain to normal residential real estate. An example would be when an appraiser assigns a tax to a property that is not taxable, such as a church.

3. INEQUALITY. This means that your property is appraised at a higher percentage for assessment than other surrounding properties. For example, if your neighbor's property is valued at $80,000.00 and has an assessed value of $20,000.00, he has a market-to-assessed-ratio of 4 to 1. If your property has a market value of $60,000.00 and an as-

sessed value of $20,000.00, you have a ratio of 3 to 1. Obviously there is an inequity here. This happens quite frequently. Unfortunately, most people don't take the time and/or effort to check on things like this, so they lose money.

You can challenge your real estate tax assessment. Each county has a Board of Assessment Review to which you can appeal. They will determine if you have a case and to what extent things can be corrected. You, of course, must file a written complaint asking for a hearing. You will, in return, receive notice of a hearing date.

To prepare your case, you should first dissect your assessor's report which is available at the assessor's office (you are allowed to review their documentation). Check the report's accuracy. For instance, is the property description correct? Does it list the correct number of rooms, sizes, etc.?

Next, check the assessment rolls and compare the assessed value with its market value. This is especially a propos if you recently purchased the home. If you bought the property at $75,000 just a few years ago and the assessor has you on the books at $100,000.00, you may well be able to convince the Board that your assessment is unfair. You should also check and make a comparison between market valuation and assessment for other properties surrounding yours. This information can be most valuable in your hearing if it shows inconsistency on your property.

If you have rental property that is in question, you will also want to review the statement of rental income and expenses, since a property's net income is a large factor in the determination of its real estate tax. Perhaps the assessor has grossly overstated the property's ability to generate income. This is a strong basis for a reduction in tax.

In your hearing, you can use experts to make a point. If you have had an appraisal made, one that differs from the assessor's, have that person testify on your behalf.

If the Board, after hearing the case, doesn't find in your favor, you can still pursue the matter in court. Here's where most people get bogged down. They believe it's not worth it to hire an attorney to pursue a few hundred dollars. After all, the attorney will cost that much and more. They are right in their thinking, but wrong in their facts.

First of all, for example, a five hundred dollar real estate tax dispute is only $500.00 for the first year. The next year it doubles and so on. In ten years it will be worth $5,000.00. That's usually true of all financial errors. They multiply! Don't forget that.

But, more importantly, one does not have to go to a lawyer to go to court. This is especially true with real estate tax matters. Obviously, if we are talking about a huge investment property, you want a lawyer. However, if you're talking about your home, and the tax reduction will amount to no more than $750.00, you qualify (in most states) for Small Claims Assessment Review.

All the information about this procedure is available at your local Small Claims Court. Many courts have a brochure for you to follow. Since this is an appeal from a prior hearing, you have the burden of proof under one of the three guidelines previously outlined. If the court finds in your favor, it will order a new assessment on your property.

Unless there is a big jump in one's real estate tax, most people will very seldom fight back. We just kind of shrug and assume it's inflation or something. We are used to all costs escalating. Our attitude regarding real estate taxes suffers because we are so often abused by taxing bodies. "You can't fight city hall" is the approach most take. The truth is, you can not only fight city hall, you can win, especially on the subject of real estate taxes.

Why? Because so many mistakes are made. The appraisals by the assessor are a joke. Office miscalculations occur. Mix-ups over what property belongs to whom happen all the time, etc., etc. I am not saying there is any sinister force at work. Rather, I'm saying that governing agencies are run by humans who make mistakes, as all humans do. Additionally, because of the nature of appraisals, we have the aspect of total subjectivity that quite often is erroneous. Any and all of these circumstances could mean you are paying more for your real estate taxes than necessary. It costs very little to find out if you're being overtaxed. It costs very little to argue the matter. Because of Small Claims, it costs very little to even appeal.

Again, a real estate tax error will follow your property every year. It multiplies. Because of that, you should do a little research on your tax assessment, whether you're satisfied or not. You review your insurance yearly. Your income tax. Your budget, etc. You should do the same with your real estate taxes. In many, many cases, there is a great deal of money to be saved. And it can accrue year after year.

HOW TO AVOID TAXES WHEN YOU SELL
YOUR HOME

Most people selling their home do so with the intent of immediately purchasing another. Under those circumstances, the issue of tax on the profit — the difference between what the seller paid for the house and the present sale price — is moot, as current law allows for a tax-free transfer if the monies from the sale, or an amount in excess of the sale price, is used to buy a new home within two years.

However, there are cases when a home is sold and the seller doesn't buy a new home. For example, when a retired couple moves to a rented condominium. They may no longer need their large home and/or have the ability, physically or financially, to take care of the house. In some instances, people not of retirement age sell a home and move to an area where housing costs are substantially below that of the area they left. In that case they are perhaps left with a small, but taxable profit. There are many housing scenarios that leave the seller with a tax consideration. This goes to work if you sell your home and make a profit and don't invest that profit in another home. In that case, you have a tax obligation.

This tax can amount to a great deal of money, because, as you know, homes have appreciated substantially over the last twenty, thirty years. Those who have lived in the same home for decades may have purchased the residence for $40,000.00, but are able to command $300,000.00 in today's market. In this example their tax would amount to, assuming a 28% tax bracket (used for illustration only), $72,800.00 ($300,00.00-$40,000.00 x .28).

Here are some things you can do to reduce the burden:

1. SUBTRACT ALL YOUR CLOSING COSTS. It is important to keep an updated mortgage file. In this case it will provide documentation regarding fees assessed when you bought the property; for example, lawyer fees, appraisal expense, bank costs, etc. These are deductible from the profit when you sell.

2. SUBTRACT THE COST OF ALL STRUCTURAL IMPROVEMENTS. All homeowners, when they make costly repairs, build additions or remodel, should keep proof of the costs. When the home is sold, you can deduct those expenses from your profit. Large projects, like a room addition, can mean a $20-$30 thousand dollar deduction from your profit.

Overlook nothing, especially if you've been in the home a long time. It's very easy to forget things under those circumstances, which is why I recommend, in addition to a mortgage file, a home improvement file.

When taking an improvement deduction against the sales's profit, you must fill out IRS Form #2119.

The two recommendations above apply to everyone, regardless of age. Those above 55 years have another benefit that may shelter all, or a substantial portion, of their potential tax. Having reached age 55, you are allowed a onetime tax shelter of $125,000 on the profit of a home sale. Let's go back to our example to see the dramatic result of applying your exemption. Subtract the $125,000.00 from the $260,000.00 profit and the 28% is only multiplied against $135,000.00, which leaves a tax of $37,800.00, or a reduction of almost 50% of the tax prior to applying the exemption. If the party had been keeping records of home improvement costs, the burden most likely would have been reduced even further.

If you are interested in more information on this subject, call the IRS (they're listed in the phone book) and ask for *Tax Information on Selling Your Home*. It's publication #523.

The tax on the profit of your home is an unfair abomination in light of the real estate taxes a home generates every year, but that's not the real issue. This is a tax that, depending on your original purchase price and the area you live, may amount to a huge sum, so it's important to exercise every legal method of reducing the liability. Sadly, most, for a variety of reasons, from forgetting its impact to thinking they're too young to worry about it, don't take precautions

along the way. Then, when they need the records, they aren't
to be found. As you can see from the above, that's a mistake.
Regardless of your present circumstances, you must treat
this matter like it's directly applicable, because, even if it
isn't now, it will be at some point. If you're prepared, you can
save thousands, perhaps tens of thousands of dollars.

JOINT TENANCY MAY BE A MISTAKE

Joint tenancy: common ownership of property by two or more people. Upon the death of one, the property passes to the survivor/co-owner without the requirement of a will or probate.

The definition of joint tenancy discloses why most married couples opt to utilize it for their property ownership, especially their house. In particular, many younger couples use joint tenancy in place of a will, thinking, as the title passes directly on death, there is no reason to go to the expense of will preparation. That conclusion is unfortunate. Additionally, even if they have a will, couples feel more secure having their investments owned by both. This is more true today, as the possibility of divorce looms larger than ever before.

Of course, joint tenancy can be used for virtually any property, and joint tenants don't have to be married. However, for the purpose of this review, we are assuming a married scenario.

At first glance, joint tenancy seems to be a logical choice for property ownership. It can simplify estate planning by eliminating probate and any court challenge of your will. So what could be wrong? Let's review a few examples that may cause you to rethink your joint tenant decision:

1. JOINT TENANCY CAN CREATE FAMILY PROBLEMS. A childless couple using joint tenancy may force their surviving families into court. For example, the husband dies and all property immediately passes to the wife. Sometime thereafter she dies. Without a will, she dies intestate; i.e., all property then passes automatically to her family. The husband's family will never receive his share of the couple's estate. The courts are bursting with this type of case. While joint tenancy may have helped the surviving spouse, it hurts the surviving families. Many individuals, especially in families where there have been remarriages, have lost their in-

heritance due to joint tenancy, and it can be assumed that in most instances that was not the intent.

2. JOINT TENANCY CAN CREATE ADDITIONAL TAXES. This is a most important issue for those who hold assets that have greatly appreciated. In most cases that pertains to a house. For example, a couple who bought their house in 1975 for $60,000.00 may have seen the value escalate to $220,000.00. If the house is held jointly, the husband's share will pass directly to the wife on his death. Later, if and when she decides to sell the house, she must pay capital gains on her half of the appreciated value, or $80,000.00 ($110,000.00-$30,000.00). But what if the title to the house had been in her husband's name and she inherited the house and its appreciation via his will? She would have no capital gains tax, assuming no added after-death appreciation, as married couples can leave estates of any size to each other tax-free. She could have saved thousands.

Some people may be thinking, how could you possibly know who will die first? Logic, based on statistical tables, dictates that in most marriages the title should be in the husband's name, as most males die substantially before their spouse. If any woman feels uncomfortable having her half of joint property titled in her husband's name, she shouldn't. Contrary to popular thinking, you cannot deny your spouse his or her half of property just because it's titled in your name. Courts don't tolerate that defense in divorce/property disputes.

If you decide not to use joint tenancy, there are steps you should take:

1. YOU AND YOUR SPOUSE MUST HAVE A WILL. As stated many times, you must have a will. Whether you make it out yourself or use a lawyer (the best option), it doesn't matter, as long as you satisfy this important requirement. Unfortunately, this doesn't discharge the matter of probate.

2. CONSIDER A REVOCABLE LIVING TRUST. This is how you solve the probate problem. For a small fee, an es-

tate attorney will draw up a revocable living trust that
transfers your properties to a trustee, of your choosing, who
manages assets for your benefit. By naming yourself as beneficiary, you receive all the benefits, including income. And,
as the trust is revocable, you can cancel it or change trustees
whenever you're so moved. The trust can be worded in such
a manner that, after your death, heirs receive the trust benefits or the trust is dissolved and property is transferred directly. In either instance probate is avoided.

I'm not implying that joint tenancy is wrong. I am, however, making a strong case that it shouldn't be thought of as
your only option. Most automatically title property in this
manner because they think it's the only and/or best way.
Both assumptions are wrong.

While there are some minor advantages to joint tenancy, there can be, as outlined above, many substantial
drawbacks. Joint tenancy can hurt your family. It can also
be a boon to the IRS. Think it over. If necessary, contact
your attorney. It's a very important subject usually given little thought.

If you make the wrong decision, your heirs will be thinking about it for a long time.

HOME IMPROVEMENTS

There are a number of sound reasons why you might consider a home improvement. Foremost would be the cost of new housing; i.e., it is often more economical to improve or expand your present property than to buy what you need. In fact, since moving can cost $10 to $20 thousand dollars (closing costs for the new house, movers, real estate broker fees for the sale of your old house, loan application fees, etc.), you may be able to remodel the kitchen or whatever for close to the same money — and that ignores the added price differential between your present home and the larger one you would be purchasing. All things considered, a home improvement may actually be cheaper than moving, and, of course, in most instances it increases the property's resale value. Additionally, by using the home improvement option, you avoid the upsetting trauma of relocating.

If you do decide on a home improvement, there are some important considerations that can either make the experience a satisfying one or a living nightmare:

1. HIRE A CONTRACTOR WITH A TRACK RECORD. While I always recommend saving money, don't try and do so by finding a handyman who believes he can handle the job. You want a home improvement contractor. Don't take his word for his ability or believe his ad in the paper or phone book. Ask for references that you can verify. Visit some of his former jobs and see the quality of the work.

Some contractors specialize in certain types of home improvements, such as kitchens. If you can find one who specializes in your needs, all the better.

Choosing the right contractor is critical! Don't rush, investigate.

2. FINDING YOUR OWN FINANCING. Many contractors will arrange your financing with their bank or lending outlet. They have the same relationship with a number of financial institutions that car dealers have. While it may sound convenient, you cannot afford anything but the lowest

cost financing, which means the contractor/bank relationship should not be considered.

The contractor doesn't care if you pay exorbitant interest. All he wants is to get paid, no matter what your ultimate cost. Additionally, many contractors, like car dealers, get a kickback from the bank for bringing in new loan business. They make a point or two, without you knowing it. On a twenty thousand dollar home improvement loan for ten years, that could cost you an additional $4,000.00 above your costs had you located your own financing.

3. HAVE A VALID CONTRACT THAT PROTECTS YOUR RIGHTS. Most contractors have a standard contract they will present — don't sign it! It was designed to protect them at your expense. These are some of the considerations you must demand:

a) The contractor should be responsible for all damage at the worksight, including vandalism.

b) The contractor should be responsible for meeting local building and zoning laws.

c) List all materials, supplies, etc., by name. That way you won't think you're getting top-of-the-line when you're not.

d) Don't let the contractor have any right to make changes without your prior written approval.

e) Make the contractor responsible for unacceptable work or problems caused by any subcontractor he hires.

f) Outline any and all verbal guarantees the contractor makes. If it's not in writing, it's going to be impossible to prove in court.

g) Outline the payment schedule so there are no misunderstandings. Normally the contractor gets 10% at the time you sign the contract. Other payments are made as the work progresses. Don't make additional payments in advance, no matter what the circumstances! Your interests are better served if you hold the contractor to the strictest interpretation of the contract payment schedule.

h) Make sure the last payment, usually the largest, is not paid until the final approval from the local building inspector is received.

i) Ensure the actual work to be done is spelled out to everyone's understanding. If possible, make the plans part of the contract proper.

j) Do not allow the common wording of "the work shall be completed in a workmanlike manner." What does that mean? It means, in case of a disagreement, the contractor will be favored in court.

As your house is perhaps your largest financial investment, you should have high standards for the quality of your home — settle for nothing less in the quality of your home improvement.

k) Have a schedule for the work to be completed, even if the work is being done in stages and you have a number of completion dates. That's the only way you can judge the contractor and his progress. It also gives you some legal muscle in case things aren't going well.

In this section, I recommend a penalty clause for the contractor not meeting his obligation. Things happen, so you don't want to be unreasonable. To that end, perhaps a penalty of $100.00 per day, starting two weeks after the scheduled completion date, would be appropriate. Regardless of what you decide, it helps if you have leverage.

l) Ensure the contractor has appropriate insurance coverage. For instance, if a workman gets hurt on the job, your homeowner's policy isn't going to cover it, so you may be sued. Can you afford that? If not, you'd better ask to see copies of all the contractor's insurance policies.

m) Insert an arbitration clause to review costs and determine who's responsible if costs start exceeding the contractor's estimates. Many customers are shocked to receive a bill far in excess of the contract, only to find out that the contractor had cost overrun rights. Know your costs up-front and don't let the contractor exceed them.

Arbitration is also good for expenses associated with unforeseen circumstances. For instance, the contractor cannot be held responsible if you have termites that have to be removed prior to workmen completing their work. Yet, there are additional costs and time lost when things like that happen. Arbitration can help if the two of you can't come to terms.

n) Have an escape clause if you're not satisfied with the work. In most cases, if you fire a contractor, no matter how bad he is, you still owe him for the job — even if you have to hire another contractor to finish the work. In court, the contractor almost always wins, unless you have protected your right to fire his firm.

o) Make the contractor responsible for all clean-up prior to being paid. You'd be surprised what a mess workers can make in and around your home.

These are just a few of the major points you need to consider when embarking on a home improvement. Obviously there will be other specifics that are germane to your circumstances. Regardless, you must understand that the experience and the final project results are almost solely the product of your planning, dedication, and homework prior to the work beginning.

Home improvements are expensive, especially once you add your financing costs. Treat the relationship with your contractor seriously. If you're unsure, although I don't think it necessary, hire a lawyer to review the contract. His fee should not exceed $250.00.

The best way to ensure your contractor doesn't become an adversary is to treat him like he is one. Be fair, be firm. Expect the worst, demand the best. Am I overselling my position? Just remember, if things turn sour, you may be left with a half-finished room addition, monthly payments on a second mortgage with a bank which doesn't care that the work isn't finished, numerous subcontractor mechanic liens on your house, a yard that has had its landscaping destroyed, fines from the local zoning board, and complaining neighbors.

YOUR INSURANCE

AMAZING NEW WAYS TO SAVE ON INSURANCE COSTS

Every one realizes that in today's sue-'em-first-ask-questions-later society, insurance is a necessity. It is also prudent as a way to replace lost, stolen, or destroyed assets, or lost earnings due to the disability or death of the principle family provider. Clearly, insurance is a financial fact of life that we all must deal with, and make a part of our overall family economics.

I will not quarrel with the need for an insurance plan. However, most families can save huge sums of money while maintaining, or even slightly improving their coverage. Where most go astray is relying on insurance companies and their salesmen when seeking insurance advice. Insurance companies sell insurance, and they will sell you as much as they can. Contrary to their sales pitch, they don't care about anything other than sales. If you need insurance advice, see your financial counselor, because insurance coverage is a financial decision, short and simple. My recommended separation of church and state, as it pertains to your insurance dollar, is the same principle as not buying investment coins from the person who gives you investment coin advice. The obvious conflict of interest will cost you. The same is true with insurance.

I would be less than honest if I didn't admit that I don't like the way insurance companies do business. Several of their tactics have brought me to this conclusion:

1. They sell through fear.

2. They oversell, especially to the less affluent — the very people who can least afford to be financially abused.

3. They promote themselves to be something they-'re not. For instance, their sales staff often call themselves "estate planners" as a way of encouraging public trust that they often abuse. They're not estate planners, they're insurance salesmen.

4. They are using their immense monetary power to misinform the public regarding the insurance crisis. Insurance companies actually have state legislators changing the laws regarding malpractice insurance, punitive awards, etc., and they have done so by using a few isolated, bizarre award cases that most reasonable persons would disagree with. The fact is, the numbers say insurance companies have an insurance crisis, not because of jury awards, but because the companies made some bad long term investments. Another fact: insurance companies are making more money than ever. Yet, they are pleading poverty in order to raise our premiums and change the already insurance-company-favorable laws to be even more so.

5. They will do whatever possible to delay or not pay rightful claims.

6. They purposely write their policies in insurancese so the general public does not understand what they have purchased (which helps them deny claims).

7. They take advantage of the elderly. Have you seen some of the ads for life insurance recently? They promise the world to those over 65, knowing full well these policies are in many cases worthless.

Insurance companies are not to be trusted. Are they a financial enemy? Sadly, the answer is yes.

Today, out of every $100.00 spent for goods and services, $13.00 is spent on insurance in some form. On average, that means most of us are spending $3,000.00 to $4,000.00 annually, which is a substantial portion of our income. Most never actually stop to consider their entire insurance package, nor do they add up all their premiums. If you have hospitalization through your employer, you probably forget that, in effect, you pay for that premium too. When you add it all up, and realize that most of us never receive one dollar in non-hospitalization related claims (until death), the insurance companies do all right. It's time to make some changes that will meet your needs while cutting the insurance company's take.

1. LIFE INSURANCE. Life insurance has three main selling points. (1) It creates an immediate estate. (2) It pays for the expenses incurred at death. (3) It is a way for many to save and invest.

Points one and two will not be debated here, as they have merit. But I caution that it serves no purpose to be over-insured. If you have a middle class life and surroundings, is it wise to insure your family in an amount that could be classified upper class? I think not. In fact, paying premiums in excess of what it would take to have your family continue their lifestyle is one way of not advancing financially. No one should be worth more dead than alive, and yet that's the basis of many life insurance plans. That's not to say that one shouldn't upgrade their life insurance coverage as they can afford it, but that's another issue.

Where most people go wrong is they don't understand that a goodly portion of a whole life policy goes to the investment portion of the contract and not any actual insurance. And since insurance companies are usually paying substantially below-market rates, you lose and they win.

What can be done? Buy only term life insurance. Term contracts are billed only for the actual insurance, which means you can save approximately 50% of the premium. Meaning you can invest the difference, or with the same dollar amount of insurance, increase your coverage substantially over what you could afford with a whole life coverage. Another recommendation is to insure yourself and others based on age and need. You want large coverage when you're young, as your family requires long-term income potential. You don't need that coverage when you're older and the kids are no longer your financial responsibility. Most families have their insurance program backwards. They have little insurance when they most need it, and when they become older and more affluent they increase their coverage dramatically. There is a stage in life when you should only have coverage to pay for burial expenses and nothing more. Unfortunately, that's when many are loading up.

If you presently have a whole life policy, you may wish to convert it, as you can take the full cash value and invest it in something more in keeping with your investment expectations. By using a term replacement, you can also, at the same time, increase your coverage. If you're older, you may wish to take the cash surrender value and use it to secure a smaller policy that you can immediately pay in full. You could also take out the cash value and use the proceeds to extend the amount of the policy itself; i.e., use the policy to pay for the policy.

The bottomline? By understanding the nuances of life insurance you can increase your coverage and save approximately 50% of what you are presently spending.

2. HOMEOWNERS INSURANCE. Homeowners insurance policies make sense because they cover in total a lot of what might be covered in individual, more costly policies (fire, and liability for example, which would be more expensive than what can be accomplished through a packaged deal). However, there are some pitfalls. Some never realize that they have an 80% co-insurance clause (you may or may not have this clause), meaning you are going to pay for 20% of the loss. It's too late to realize that after your home burns down.

During high inflation, and usually after a tragedy, some people find out they didn't make allowance for higher replacement costs. There are policies that take yearly inflationary adjustments into account, which increases your coverage. Or, if you can afford it and your property warrants, consider coverage that includes "replacement value."

For the sake of your financial sanity, make a detailed inventory of your belongings, including serial numbers where applicable. If you have a problem, I can assure you that your company is going to try everything possible to low-ball your claim. The only way to counteract their position is to have a file (kept outside the home) proving the contents and their worth. This technique can save you thousands, not in premiums, but in lost claim money.

The biggest money saver in this area is understanding you may have over-insured your home, and are paying overly inflated premiums because of it. Most have their home insured for market value. That is to say if your home has a resale value of $100,000.00, that's what you have it insured for (or possibly more). What you forget is, a substantial part of your market value is the property the home sits on, and that doesn't burn or get destroyed in a disaster. A typical home having a market value of $100,000.00 would break down as having a lot value of $30,000.00 and a home value of $70,000.00. Consequently, you're $30,000.00 over-insured. You should only have insurance for the replacement of the structure(s), not the market value of the property.

One final note: Unless you have a replacement policy (which I don't necessarily recommend for everyone), the insurance company will only pay the depreciated value of your home inventory. When setting your limits regarding this subject, most say it will cost X dollars to replace the furniture, and they insure on that basis. Then they have a fire and lose everything. Chances are, they will receive only a portion of their loss. Depending on the time that has passed, they may only get twenty five cents on the dollar. The point is, on depreciating assets, you should be aware that you are probably paying for a benefit that is non-existent. Adjust accordingly.

You should be able to save at least 30% on your premiums without disrupting your present coverage.

3. CAR INSURANCE. Car insurance is necessary for all the obvious reasons. But, there are savings to be gained. If you have a fairly new car, make sure your collision coverage

has as high a deductible as you can legitimately afford. Low deductibles make for grossly overpriced premiums, and in fact, you have to have several accidents just to break even on the premiums — no joke intended.

You can achieve savings by keeping your driving-to-work miles lower than the company's limit (usually ten miles). Work mileage is one of the main factors used in figuring your premium. If you have farther than that to drive, you may wish to consider public transportation, since work miles that are over the insurance company's limit can increase your premium by as much as 30%.

City dwellers should try and establish a residence address in a rural area if legally possible. The difference in premiums here can be as much as 50%.

The biggest savings that can be realized with car insurance is dropping your collision insurance as soon as it is feasible. Usually this will be around the third or fourth year you own your car. Remember, the insurance company is only going to give you book-value as a replacement. It doesn't matter what you think the car is worth, or what it will cost to replace; all you're going to get is the black or blue book value in actual dollars. Collision insurance is expensive, especially with the cost of repairs today, and I can guarantee you are going to be disappointed to find out you have been paying premiums for years on a car, only to receive very little in return when you have an accident. As opposed to fixing the car, they will "total" it, and hand you a check for perhaps nickels on the dollar.

Bottomline: When your car starts to show some age, consider dropping your collision coverage, and gain a savings of 30% to 50%.

4. HOSPITALIZATION. This type of coverage is so expensive most individuals can't afford it, which is why I recommend a group plan. Fortunately, many have such a plan through their employer. A major recommendation: read that policy now, before you have to. Many find out that their policy is inadequate, but usually they find out too late. If yours

is one that doesn't meet your needs, and possibly that of other employees, talk to your boss. Although your employer will tell you your insurance is a bonus or perk for working there, you pay for that coverage. Your salary takes into account all your benefits; i.e., they are covertly or overtly considered when the cost per employee is calculated, which means your take home pay is reduced by the amount of your benefits. So, while you don't get a bill, you do pay the premium, and as such you should have some say as to the coverage.

For those of you who don't have a group policy, find a group you can join. One I know of (I don't recommend this firm or any others) is Co-op America, 2100 M St., NW, Suite 310, Washingon, D.C. 20063. Phone: 1-800-424-COOP. 1-202-8772-5307. They offer a group policy once you join. Their membership is minimal.

If you have individual hospitalization coverage, you can save approximately 30 to 40% by joining a group. If you have a group policy through work, you can save an untold amount by checking your coverage before the fact and demanding changes if needed. If you don't have coverage, you can save your finances and perhaps your life (some hospitals will not treat even trauma patients if they don't have hospitalization insurance) by joining an independent group.

Insurance is important. Any portion of our spendable income that approximates 13% spent on goods and services deserves attention. More importantly than the savings, you must take time to understand what you actually have. Chances are you don't have what you think you have in some area of your insurance coverage, and that could be devastating.

Lastly, remember that your insurance company is just that, your insurance company. They are not your friends, nor is your agent. They sell insurance. As nice as they both can be, when you have a major claim or problem, you are going to see exactly how adversarial they can become, and just how fast that can occur. Remember too, investing money through your insurance policy is an investing mistake that rates a ten on the mistake meter.

KEY HEALTH INSURANCE QUESTIONS

Everyone needs health insurance. Over and above the significance of the medical considerations, (i.e., without insurance many hospitals will deny even emergency services), it can mean the difference between living or dying financially. With hospital beds running as high as $1,200.00 a day, its importance is not debatable. One major illness and your future, and that of your family, can be lost. But this discussion, while consequential, is not the focus of my concern, as I assume my readers, realizing its priority, have health insurance. But, do you have the right health insurance? My guess is, unless you recently had an illness that forced you to check your policy, you probably don't know.

There are a series of questions you must ask, whether you're buying a policy now or are reviewing and/or updating your existing coverage:

1. WHEN DOES MY COVERAGE START? After purchasing a policy, far too many people have been devastated to find, after being rushed to the hospital, their policy was not yet in effect.

2. IS EVERYONE IN MY FAMILY COVERED? Don't take this for granted. Read the policy carefully.

3. ARE THERE AGE LIMITATIONS? For example, at what age are your children no longer covered under the umbrella of your policy? And what happens when you reach retirement? Can you convert the policy, or are you simply dropped? Better find out now.

4. CAN THE INSURANCE COMPANY, AT THEIR OWN DISCRETION, CANCEL MY POLICY? Too many health insurance companies have too many reasons/excuses to cancel the policies of people who are experiencing expensive health care problems. The last thing you need at that point is a letter from your insurance company informing you you're on your own.

5. WHAT CONDITIONS ARE EXCLUDED FROM THE POLICY? Many policies have exclusions that may, at some

point in the future, affect you. Don't assume that all conditions and illnesses are covered, because they're probably not.

6. ARE PRE-EXISTING CONDITIONS COVERED? This can be a major issue for those with existing conditions, especially if they have been forced to change companies; i.e., you can get caught in the middle of the transfer with no coverage. Ask if the condition will be covered and when the coverage goes into effect. Pre-existing conditions normally are covered, but only after a substantial waiting period.

7. ARE DIAGNOSTIC TESTS COVERED? Some policies deny payments for diagnostic tests. As you know, these can be very expensive, too expensive for you to bear the cost yourself. This is an important aspect of your health care — your policy must include diagnostic coverage or you're in trouble.

8. WHAT IS THE DEDUCTIBLE? For most, from a cost/benefit standpoint, it is probably better to have the highest deductible you can easily afford. That lowers the cost of the policy. Regardless of what you decide, you must know the dollar deductible limits and how they are applied.

9. AFTER THE DEDUCTIBLE, WHAT PERCENTAGE OF THE BILL IS MY RESPONSIBILITY? The trouble here is, even if the consumer knows the answer, they seldom realize, until it's too late, what that means in dollars and cents. For example, it's not uncommon for a policy, after the deductible of $X, to pay 80% of covered expenses. Your responsibility of 20% sounds so innocuous. But, if you have a major medical bill of one or two hundred thousand dollars you're talking a personal financial crisis.

10. WHAT ARE THE MAXIMUMS? You need to know the most the insurance will pay under major medical, and does that coverage apply to each separate illness or accident?

Further, once you've reached the maximum, are you covered if the problem reoccurs, or is there a waiting period?

11. DOES THE COVERAGE ADEQUATELY REFLECT HEALTH CARE COSTS IN OUR AREA? If you live

in a rural community you need coverage of $X. If you live in
New York City, you may need coverage of two or three times
$X. For example, in many towns the per day hospital bed ex-
pense is approximately $500.00. In New York City, a hospi-
tal bed alone can cost $1,200.00 per day. Everything else —
all medicines, etc. — is extra. That's why it's essential that
you have this protection! Sadly, some people are underinsured. You must match coverage to circumstances. Remember this important consideration when you move to a new lo-
cale.

12. IS THERE A PROVISION THAT LIMITS MY EX-
POSURE? Some policies have a stop/loss or out-of-pocket
limitation. This is an excellent idea for all the obvious reasons.

13. EXACTLY WHAT SERVICES ARE COVERED?
For instance:

a. How many in-hospital days are covered and at
what cost?

b. Does the policy pay for nurses, X-rays, medica-
tions, laboratory costs, operating rooms, etc.?

c. What operations are covered and is coverage full
or partial? This is crucial, as insurance companies
try to deny paying for many life-saving operations
by terming them experimental. Check this aspect
of your coverage.

14. IS THIS COMPANY LICENSED IN MY STATE?
As nonsensical as this may sound, should you have a problem with the company, it's important your state's insurance
board/department be able to assist. It's easier for them and
you if the company has assets and offices in your state. Then
too, it's probably not a wise idea to be doing business with an
insurance company that hasn't bothered, for whatever reason, to become licensed in your state.

As noted earlier, my readers understand the importance
of health insurance. But having health insurance is only one
aspect of the equation. You must know the specifics of your

coverage. This is especially true if you have health insurance through work. Have you looked closely at your policy? Can you answer the above questions without looking? If not, you'd better inventory your policy. It's too late once you or a family member check into the hospital. Unfortunately, as with many financial transactions, the consumer often only gets half the job done. With health care, that usually means they have coverage — they just aren't acquainted with the details. That may be the most important financial mistake they ever make.

INSURANCE CLAIMS

Insurance companies try, whenever possible, to refuse claims. They have large departments charged with that ethically questionable goal. If they can find any reason, however remote, they will deny you monetary assistance. I mention this now so you'll remember what you're up against when you look to your insurance company for help.

Realizing the insurance company's mind-set makes it incumbent on you to ensure you do nothing that might jeopardize your claim.

It has to be noted that many people are embarrassed to file an insurance claim. Don't be. You pay overpriced premiums for protection. It would be foolish not to use a service for which you've paid dearly.

Then there are those who are worried that the insurance company may raise their rates if they file a claim. While that's possible, and perhaps even likely, it shouldn't dissuade you from exercising your insurance rights when you've experienced a loss.

If you take the two above concerns, embarrassment and fear of raised rates, and take them to their logical extreme, you would have to conclude that these people shouldn't bother with insurance of any kind except catastrophic. Clearly one shouldn't take that position. That leaves us with an undeniable bottomline: if you have a claim, file it.

Here, therefore, are some tips that will help you be successful with your claim:

1. READ ALL YOUR POLICIES CAREFULLY. Know what coverage you have. If you're not sure if you're covered for a specific loss, file a claim anyway. You have nothing to lose, and you might be the surprised beneficiary of a subjective opinion in your favor.

2. KEEP EVERY DOCUMENT THAT MIGHT HAVE A BEARING ON YOUR CLAIM. Throw nothing away. An insurance company will return forms if a single blank isn't

filled in. Think of what they'll do if you don't have a bill or estimate. Documentation is extremely important with health claims. When you go to the doctor or hospital, grab every piece of paper with your name on it.

Before sending in your claim, make copies for your home file in case the claim gets lost along the way.

One missing or lost document can cost you months of aggravation. Remember, insurance companies want to deny your claim. Even if they pay it, the longer they hold onto the money, the longer they get to use the funds for their investment purposes. Insurance companies are masters at using the float of delayed claims.

3. KEEP A DIARY OF THE EVENTS THAT SPAWN-ED THE CLAIM, AS WELL AS THOSE SUBSEQUENT. Include all the conversations you have with the insurance company representatives. Take names, phone numbers, etc. You may need this record, especially if your claim is refused.

4. IF YOU'RE UNSURE OF WHAT TO DO, ASK FOR HELP. Don't be afraid to ask for assistance in filling out your claim forms. Call the company's Customer Service Department. They can be helpful in many situations. This won't help you with the claims representative, but at least you won't be delayed on a technicality.

Of course, even more important than the above is what to do if the company refuses your claim. Most just throw up their hands and take no for an answer. You cannot afford to do that, especially with a substantial claim you believe should have been covered. At a minimum you should:

1. Write the supervisor of the department that denied your claim. Explain your position and ask for additional review. If that doesn't work, go over the supervisor's head to his or her boss and so on, until you get to the president. Keep copies of all your letters and the company's responses. You'll need them for the next step.

2. If your in-house campaign isn't successful, send a copy of your file, along with a cover letter/ complaint, to your state's insurance commissioner. This office is normally located at the state capitol. Call your state's telephone Information Operator or the Information Desk if you can't locate the office.

The insurance commissioner's representative will review the matter and correspond with your insurer. This may cause the company to rethink their position. If they have committed a gross error or misdeed, the commissioner's office may force compliance, which would be beneficial to your case. At the very least, after receiving a complaint from the commissioner (which is kept on file with other complaints against the insurance company), the insurer will have paid a price for their decision to deny your claim.

It's too bad people don't fight insurance companies. If they did, many more would receive positive responses to their claims. As it is now, insurers know they have nothing to lose by denying even legitimate claims.

INSURANCE YOU DON'T NEED

Insurance companies take advantage of people. Contrary to their public position of consumer service, they are in the business of making huge profits any way they can. That's not to imply that insurance itself is not worthwhile. Quite the contrary. It's an excellent vehicle that assists us in planning for the good and bad events that most assuredly will occur. The complaint with insurance is not with the concept, it's with the prostitution of the concept by insurance companies.

As we've discussed, insurance companies don't deliver what they promised when you bought your policy. What's more, even when you do have a legitimate claim, they will try and deny it by whatever means possible. And, since insurance policies are written in insurancese, loopholes that allow claim denials are not hard for the insurance company to find.

Insurance companies are also in the process of using undue influence to change our legal system. For instance, they have an expensive publicity campaign, aimed at our legislators, to have states place limits on awards for medical malpractice and manufacturer's product liability. They use examples in their press releases that outline rare cases where perhaps a jury did offer excessive monetary punitive damages, and then draw the conclusion that all such cases are excessive. What they never mention is, in almost all cases where we all could agree that a jury was excessive, the award is later substantially reduced by a higher court. And insurance companies ignore the fact that such cases are not representational of most jury awards. Regardless of the size of an award, how much money is fair payment for being in a wheelchair the rest of your life? The point being, you can't look at one award and make a determination about the system. You have to intimately know the case and the ultimate monetary resolution. Insurance companies continually attack the courts, not for the purpose of changing the law per se, but rather to justify the escalating cost of every type of insurance coverage. Unfortunately, their conspiratorial attack is working, as more and more states are doing the bidding of the industry.

The real issue should be a focus on insurance and what it is or is not providing those who pay premiums. But, the insurance industry can't afford a public audit, so it keeps focusing our lawmaker's attention on the public — in effect saying, we are at fault for the insurance mess. Nothing could be further from the truth. Look at the bottomline. Insurance companies are constantly pleading poverty, because of "outrageous" damage awards, but I ask, what is the largest building in almost every major city? That's right, an insurance company's corporate headquarters building. Further, who has one of the larger, or largest, account(s) in almost every major money-center bank? That's right, an insurance company. The question has to be asked, if we are to believe the insurance industry and there is no profit in most insurance coverages, where is all their money coming from? The insurance industry position is a sham. Remember, we're not talking about insurance, as that has obvious merit. The industry likes to ignore, or mute, the difference between insurance and insurance industry. Here is another important truth. Much of the so-called insurance crisis has nothing to do with insurance. It's a result of insurance companies making bad investments over the last twenty years. That's where their losses have been. But they can't change that. So, they are making up the difference by going after the consumer through higher and higher premiums for less and less coverage.

Probably nothing makes clearer their attack than the plethora of what I call, "junk insurance." Let's look at just a few.

1. AIR TRAVEL INSURANCE. These premiums are almost 100% profit to the insurance company. Why? Because air travel is almost 100% safe. You have a greater chance of winning a lottery than you do crashing in a plane. Statistically your family's odds of collecting, even if you're a daily

air traveler, are practically nil. More importantly, if an accident does occur, your family will have plenty of people to sue. The plane's manufacturer, possibly the airport, the airline, etc. The bottomline is, you're already insured when you get on a plane. You don't need air insurance.

2. CANCER, MUGGING, OR OTHER PARTICULAR EVENT INSURANCE. As we all have concerns regarding cancer, or being attacked on the street, these are perfect events for the insurance companies to use to play on our fears. The premiums on these types of coverages are high, in some cases extremely high. Yet, what are you actually buying? If you get cancer, suffer medical expense due to a mugging, or whatever, you are already covered through your present medical coverage. If the worst happens, you have life insurance. If you have specific fears in this regard, increase your life or health insurance coverage. General comprehensive coverages are far superior to specific events coverage.

3. LIFE INSURANCE FOR UNMARRIED PERSONS. As silly as this may sound, millions of individuals have substantial life insurance coverage and no married family. This is truly a living monument to the selling ability of insurance agents, but it has no real value to the insured. If you are unmarried and die, no one's economic wellbeing is threatened. So why are you insured? This same principle would be true with a dual-income family having no children.

Take the premiums you would have spent and start an investment program. You'll be thousands ahead.

4. LIFE INSURANCE FOR KIDS. As sad as anyone's passing is, especially a child's, from a monetary standpoint it makes no sense to have them insured, because, here too, who's economic wellbeing is threatened? No one's, so save the premium expense.

5. RENTAL CAR INSURANCE. Provided that your automobile insurance covers damage for any car you are driving, including a rental car, this is coverage you don't need. Check your policy, especially if you are a frequent car renter. For most of us, this is coverage we already have (if you don't

have car insurance, or if your coverage excludes rentals, check to see if the credit card you're using gives automatic coverage). For those few who don't have such personal coverage, you have little choice but to buy renter's car insurance, even with its high daily cost.

6. CREDIT LIFE, DISABILITY, AND MORTGAGE LOAN INSURANCE. These are overpriced and of little value. Depending on the loan vehicle, the premium may be subject to a finance charge, which obviously adds to a high cost. In each case you are, in effect, insuring the lending institution, because the monies will go directly to them to pay off the loan balance. Your family cannot use those funds as they see fit. If you really see a need to insure a lending obligation, raise your life insurance coverage a like amount. It will be substantially cheaper for the same dollar coverage.

7. VACATION INSURANCE. As hard as this may be to believe, many people pay substantial premiums to "insure" their vacation. For example, if it rains beyond a certain limit you can receive a predetermined refund of your expenses. As disappointing as a ruined vacation can be, it is not worth insuring yourself against the possibility. Save your money.

8. GLASSES OR CONTACT LENSES INSURANCE. For the cost of the premiums, you can almost buy another pair of glasses. This type of insurance is a perfect example of insuring something that is not, by itself, a financial burden if it's lost, stolen, or broken. With the cost of insurance today, it's not advisable to insure anything you can comfortably afford to replace.

9. PET INSURANCE. Health insurance for a pet is not a worthwhile expense, because the premiums are so high as to eclipse most vet bills. Your benefits, even if you do get to use the coverage (which is highly unlikely), are usually less than the premiums you've paid. It makes no sense on any level.

10. $50, $75, or $100 A DAY HEALTH INSURANCE. These policies are sold thorugh fear, since everyone knows that the cost of health insurance is getting to the point

where, regardless of your insurance coverage, no one can afford to be sick. But, if you read the policy closely, they offer less than you could receive if you took the premium amount and increased your present health insurance. This amounts to gap-insurance, which is very, very costly.

11. LIFE INSURANCE REGARDLESS OF HEALTH OR AGE. These policies are sold through the mail or on late night television. Unfortunately, they manage to catch the attention of those who need help the most, but can afford it the least. Most policies, while they will not refuse coverage, have a clause that denies a benefit for anything other than previously paid premiums for the first two years. Because the elderly or ill are the target market, the insurance company has a win/win proposition. If the insured passes away in the first two years, the insurance company simply gives back money they've had investment use of for two years. If the insured passes away after two years, they have made enough in general premiums to cover the expense. This is very expensive coverage. When it's being sold, however, it sounds inexpensive. Look closely. The ad doesn't specify what amount you're being insured for, it simply refers to X dollars per unit. The per unit is usually a very small amount (a few thousand dollars). Therefore, the $5.00 or $10.00 per unit, per month, is actually substantially more than many realize.

The consumer is at ever-expanding risk with the insurance industry. Your insurance education must keep up with the insurance industry's attempts to take more and more of your money. Trust no one on this subject, especially your insurance agent. His job is to sell insurance. Your job is only to buy insurance that provides actual cost-effective benefit to your family. For those of you who doubt the insurance industry's ulterior motives, the above listing of completely useless coverages should help make the point.

Again, my complaint is not with insurance, it's with insurance companies. A final cost-saving note: buy life insurance, health insurance, auto insurance, disability insurance, and homeowners insurance, and take the highest deductibles you can afford on each. Other, specific need coverages you may require can be added, as a rider, to these basic comprehensive policies at little cost.

YOU AND THE LAW

ARBITRATION

Arbitration is normally thought of in the context of a labor/management dispute. That's no longer the case.

With the high cost of acquiring legal representation, and the extended length of time it takes for a court case to be resolved, another, less expensive, less time-consuming method of resolving every day matters had to be instituted. It's called Alternative Dispute Resolution (ADR). ADR is either mediation or arbitration.

Arbitration is more formal than mediation, but less so than litigation. Each participant in the dispute submits their side of the case, in writing, to the arbitrator(s) — there may be as many as five arbitrators per dispute. At the hearing, each side has the opportunity to present witnesses and cross-examine all those who testify. The arbitrator(s) can also ask questions during the process. While most people represent themselves in an arbitration hearing, in complicated cases you may wish to avail yourself of an attorney. This is permitted, but in my mind, self-defeating; i.e., if you need a lawyer, you probably should be in formal litigation, not arbitration.

The arbitrators are people completely neutral in the matter before them and, whenever possible, they try and persuade both sides to be reasonable and see the other person's point of view. Quite often, at the hearing, they can arrange a settlement without making a decision per se. However, when that's not possible, they resolve the matter at hearing's end, or in writing within a few days. In today's legal environment, arbitration is unbelievably expeditious.

There are two types of arbitration, binding and nonbinding. Before entering an arbitration process, you'll be informed of which yours is and then you can decide whether or not you wish to proceed.

Binding arbitration, while appealable on points of law, is not disputable, and both sides have to abide by the decision rendered.

Non-binding arbitration, of course, is just the opposite. If you don't like the verdict, you can challenge the decision. However, to stop those who will abuse the system, most arbitration has a disincentive if you appeal. That being a penalty, for instance paying the other side's expenses, if your appeal is not successful.

Why should you know about and consider arbitration? Because:

1. It resolves disputes almost immediately.

2 It resolves disputes at no or low cost.

3. It allows you to resolve disputes that otherwise, due to time and money considerations, might have to be left unresolved.

4. It allows you to present your dispute to arbitrators who have a professional background in solving the exact type of problem you are experiencing.

Arbitration Associations:

1. AMERICAN ACADEMY OF DIVORCE CONCILIATORS

P.O. Box 2246
Claremont, CA 91711

2. AMERICAN ARBITRATION ASSOCIATION

140 W. 51st St., 10th Floor
New York, NY 10020

(Has over 20 offices throughout the country. They arbitrate civil and property disputes.)

3. AMERICAN AUTOMOBILE ASSOCIATION (AAA)

8111 Gatehouse Rd.
Falls Church, VA 22047

(All AAA auto repair shops are obligated to agree to the arbitration ruling or lose their AAA rating. The arbitration is non-binding on the consumer.)

4. AUTOMOBILE ARBITRATION

(Contact the manufacturer of the car in question and ask for their arbitration brochure. It will outline the parameters of the process. Most major car companies have such non-binding avenues available. For instance, Ford, GM, and Chrysler have consumer arbitration divisions. Because of the obvious conflict of interest, use caution.)

5. STANDING COMMITTEE ON DISPUTE RESOLUTION

American Bar Association
1800 M Street NW
Washington, DC 20036

(Write if you wish a free copy of their directory that outlines all court related ADR programs.)

6. COUNCIL OF BETTER BUSINESS BUREAUS

1515 Wilson Blvd.
Arlington, VA 22209

(The Better Business Bureau offers arbitration for most consumer complaints. Their arbitration is usually binding on both parties. Contact your local office for details.)

7. NATIONAL INSTITUTE OF DISPUTE RESOLUTION

1901 L Street NW
Washington, DC 20036

(They offer a free directory on all ADR organizations, civil and court related.)

8. SOCIETY OF PROFESSIONALS IN DISPUTE RESOLUTION

1730 Rhode Island Ave. NW, Ste. 909
Washington, DC 20036

(This professional organization is of no use to the consumer in actual arbitration matters. I mention it because you may write and ask for their free newsletter and directory, both of which you'll find informative.)

I have low regard for our court system. On all levels, criminal and civil, it no longer works. Most objective professionals, liberal and conservative alike, agree on that unfortunately conspicuous point.

I also have low regard for most attorneys. Too many are incompetent. For their own personal financial gain, they have perverted the best conceived court system ever devised. It is no coincidence that fully two thirds of all attorneys in the world practice in the United States. It is not happenstance that most politicians, who continue to make law profitable to the legal community, are former or practicing lawyers. It is not a quirk of fate that most attorneys are exceptionally affluent. The point being, the system doesn't work, and those who could make needed changes are the very people who stand to profit the most by retaining the status quo. Which is why I offer the arbitration alternative. Justice is worth fighting for, and arbitration is one method of getting to the bottomline without being ensnared by the courts.

PARALEGALS

I hope you never have to use a lawyer in an adversarial dispute, but if such events occur, you have little choice. You will more than likely avail yourself of an attorney. Hopefully one who specializes in the type of case at issue. That makes sense.

But what about the other times when you need legal services, but don't actually have a case per se? For instance, an incorporation for your small business. Do you really need a lawyer? Perhaps, perhaps not. That's for you to decide. Yet, while you may wish to avoid lawyers and their high-priced, more than likely overpriced, fees, you are still aware that you need assistance. Make a mistake here and you can have big problems down the line with the state and the federal government, not to mention the IRS. So, am I recommending a lawyer? Yes, if you feel the need. No, if you don't.

But that doesn't have to be the end of the discussion. There is a legal alternative. It's called the paralegal.

Paralegals are people who are not members of the bar, yet perform a variety of legal tasks that may be processed by those not empowered to practice law. You might call them legal-paper-shufflers, and I don't mean that unkindly. The truth is, the average general practitioner attorney is nothing more than a high-priced paper-shuffler. So, you have a choice. A reasonably priced paper-shuffler or one who costs two, three, perhaps four times as much to complete the same task. The end result will be the same. The only thing in debate is how much you are going to pay. That's why I like paralegals.

Let's look at the types of services paralegals can provide:

1. UNCONTESTED DIVORCES AND ANNULMENTS. These are cases where both parties are in agreement. The only thing that needs to be done is satisfy the legal requirements.

2. BANKRUPTCIES. (Pages 45 and 67) BKs are almost entirely a paper matter. Unless yours is exceptionally complicated and/or contested, a paralegal meets your needs.

3. INCORPORATIONS. As mentioned above, incorporations are a perfunctory matter that simply need someone who understands the requirements. For most, incorporations are a fill-in-the-blank proposition, yet people spend thousands for an attorney to complete a job that involves nothing more than a few dollars.

4. ADOPTIONS. I am referring to consenting adoptions. Again, a fill-in-the-blanks matter that a paralegal can accomplish at a fraction of the cost an attorney will charge.

5. DEBT COLLECTIONS. Paralegals can perform quite well in this field. It doesn't matter if you're considering action for monies owed you for services, sales, interest, child support, or whatever. Debt collection, assuming a valid and legal claim, is a matter of knowing what forms to fill out and where to place your claim.

6. WILLS. Do you know that many attorneys in every major market use a computer program to prepare most of their will work? They simply ask you the questions and feed the information into their program. The computer does the rest. Of course, you'll never know that, but that's what happens quite often. Then they hand you a bill for a small fortune for their so-called expertise. Paralegals have access to the same programs. Except their charges are usually reasonable.

7. SIMPLE REAL ESTATE TRANSFERS. This involves transfers of property from a friend to another, or through various family members. Uncomplicated real estate transfers between buyer and seller that are in complete agreement on all aspects of the transaction also qualify for a paralegal's consideration.

8. TENANT'S RIGHTS DISPUTES. Most lawyers don't want to be bothered by this area of the law. It doesn't pay enough, so if they'll take your case they may severely over-

charge to make up for their aggravation. Paralegals want the work. This holds true for evictions also.

There are other legal actions a paralegal can help you with. Probate, partnerships, social security claims, name changes, etc., to name a few. A rule of thumb is, if it's not a disputed claim or case, chances are a paralegal can complete the work.

Where can you find a paralegal? In most areas, you can find them in the phone book. If you can't locate one, call the National Association for Independent Paralegals at 1-800-542-0034. While it isn't their job to locate paralegals for the public, they may direct you to one in your area.

Paralegals are becoming a force in the legal world. They have established a foothold in almost every major market. They, like all service businesses, have their share of good professionals and bad performers. Certainly you have to use normal caution when establishing a relationship. However, once that is done to your satisfaction, I believe you'll find paralegals extremely rewarding financially. They get the job done at a small portion of the cost normally associated with legal work.

One final thought. Lawyers hate paralegals. They have done everything possible to try and prohibit them from entering the extremely profitable field of standard legal transactions. They will continue to wage their fight to stop us, the public, from acquiring reasonably priced legal services.

I like the concept of paralegals. The fact that lawyers hate them makes clear that my judgement is correct.

THINK TWICE ABOUT SUING

You should always pursue your legal rights. There are many ways to accomplish that goal without using an expensive lawyer. Yet, there are cases and circumstances where you may have to consider filing a suit that will call for an attorney.

It's a fact of life, not every legal problem you will encounter can be solved in small claims court. Over and above the monetary restrictions of small claims, you, should you be under criminal indictment, would be wise to hire the best legal defense possible. Once things become that serious, it is extremely important for you to understand that your guilt or innocence depends, not on your guilt or innocence, but rather on what the jury or judge perceives to be the truth. That perception will be determined on the skill of your counsel. Even in court, you get what you pay for.

Let's put criminal law aside, though, as that is not a financial matter per se. That leaves us with a civil case that is either serious in nature or financially in excess of the small claims limitations.

Most would agree at this point in the nation's history that suing, or "having your day in court," is fashionable. The reason is, we have a society which has come to believe everything that happens to an individual is someone else's fault. Further, that someone else should pay for their mistake. I am not making light of legitimate cases, just making an observation. Our court system is overloaded, not because of cases that have merit, but rather because of cases that are based solely on the possibility of making a fortune in the court-lottery game. To prove the point that our country is sue happy, remember, the United States has more attorneys than the rest of the world combined. I am not talking about lawyers-per-thousand or any ratio, just straight numbers.

Lets look at the ability to sue in the light of finances and finances only. As anyone who has sued or been involved in the courts can tell you, it costs money to proceed with litigation. Even if you're on contingency, there are out-of-pocket lawyer expenses, and these can add up quickly. Most people are stunned when they get their legal bill. Regardless of what they thought they were getting in terms of representation, they universally are disappointed in the amount they owe for services they probably are not satisfied with. That means there are some specifics to look at before getting involved in the courts.

Forget principle, although I applaud you, should you have the ability to pursue a matter solely on that basis; financially, principle means nothing in a law suit. Let's review the legal bottomline.

1. WHAT WILL YOU GET IF YOU WIN? So many times a plaintiff will win a case, only to find out the defendant has insufficient assets to meet the award. What happens? The defendant files bankruptcy and you're out of luck.

This happens in small claims quite often; i.e., the award is just the start of the process. You still have to collect.

In any case that involves finances, your determination of whether or not to continue should be based on monetary considerations. Why pursue it if the defendant can't pay if you win? You're wasting your time and money in a situation like this, yet it happens every day. Before following up on a case, you must determine if the person or company can be held financially accountable should you win. If not, or if things look marginal, forget it.

2. WILL YOUR CASE BALANCE OUT YOUR LOSS OF TIME AND POSSIBLE EMBARRASSMENT? Court cases are public record, and a good attorney for the other side might ask questions you might not like to answer in front of hundreds of people, and/or see in the local paper. Also, remember that the courts are a bottomless pit; i.e., once you start a case, even a simple case, you may be looking at years, many years, until resolution. I can't stress enough that you have to be aware of what you are getting into. For most, it is a nightmare they wish they had never started.

3. WHAT WILL BE LEFT IN DOLLARS AND CENTS
(assuming the defendant is able to pay)?

Your attorney (we're not talking about small claims cases) will hand you a sizable bill for his or her services. On contingency, they usually receive one-third if settled out of court, or one-half if a trial is necessary. That's ignoring the monster additional bill you'll get for sundry associated expenses.

The result? You better be planning on, no, you better be sure that you will win and win big before becoming involved. Again, I am refusing to acknowledge principle. We're talking money, and that says most cases, regardless of their merit, are a very bad bet. When the dust settles, only a small portion of the winners actually walk away with anything. The lawyers do quite nicely, thank you, but that's another subject.

I believe one should fight back when it's called for. Don't misconstrue this section. However, there are plenty of other ways, financially superior ways, to receive justice.

1. LEARN HOW TO RESOLVE MATTERS DIRECTLY.
Once you learn the nuances of filing complaints, etc., you'll quickly see that the courts are, in most instances, a poor alternative to personal initiative.

2. REMEMBER SMALL CLAIMS COURT.
Probably all your legal problems can be solved here. If at all possible, use this individual forum as opposed to hiring an attorney. Oftentimes you may wish to file for less than you're owed just to be able to use small claims. For instance, if you have a $3,500.00 claim, but your state has a $2,500.00 limit on small claims, you will be money ahead, assuming you feel comfortable in the small claims environment, to use small claims and lose the difference of $1,000.00. Believe me, your attorney would have taken that much and more for doing what you probably can do yourself.

3. CONSIDER ARBITRATION. The costs, if there are any, are minimal, and there is virtually no limit on the type of dispute that can be arbitrated.

Also important is that many feel more at ease in this surrounding than they would have in court. That increases your chances of making a good presentation, which is critical to your success.

There are times and circumstances where an attorney is required. I want to make you aware of my research on the subject of whether or not you should sue. When asked whether, given the chance, they would do it over again, fully three out of four plaintiffs I questioned stated they would not sue even under the exact same circumstances.

That's a strong indictment of our court system. Those who seek legal redress for a grievance are overwhelmingly disappointed in what the lawyers have done to what was once a system we could be proud of. The courts have failed on almost every level, or so says the majority who have entered either the criminal or civil door.

I am devoted to your financial interests, and in that light I say, without reservation, think long and hard about suing. Try and look at the bottomline objectively, without the prejudice of principle, because right or wrong, your day-in-court may substantially impact your finances in a most negative way.

If, after deliberation, you still decide to proceed, at least, win or lose, you will know that you weren't monetarily defeated by an error in judgement. Most, when realizing they can win and still financially lose, will opt to press on with more important matters that offer greater potential for gain.

LAWYER RIP-OFFS

Because we are a litigious society, lawyers are a necessary evil, so you must know how to properly employ their services. The most common error consumers make is allowing the attorney to be the dominant player in the relationship. Better you see him or her as hired help. That, after all, is a true reflection of the bottomline.

Lawyers are a lot like banks. They know how to intimidate their clients. And that intimidation is then used to financially abuse those clients.

Although it would be impossible to list all the possible exploitations here, I'd like to give you a few examples of lawyer rip-offs:

1. THE BILLING UNIT METHOD OF CHARGING. The attorney takes whatever he or she charges per hour and applies that to the nearest quarter hour. For instance, if their per-hour charge is $100.00, they charge $25.00 per quarter-hour. They assess that fee every time you contact them. In this case, if you call and talk for 5 minutes, you will be charged the minimum quarter-hour fee of $25.00. Talk for 17 minutes and you'll be charged $50.00. It can quadruple the lawyers per-hour stated fee. And you can see what it could do to your bill.

The way to stop this form of abuse is to ensure that your contract with the lawyer states, assuming you don't have a flat fee agreement, that you will be charged for actual minutes only.

2. LAWYERS MAKE MONEY ABUSING TIME. Unless you have a flat fee agreement (which in many cases I recommend), the longer the lawyer takes to resolve your case, the more money he or she can charge. This is done all too often.

In many cases, these delaying tactics don't matter; i.e., your work isn't time-sensitive. But, more often than not, time is important. Even in non-court matters — loan closings, contract signings, estate settlements, etc. — time counts. You need to get things done. Chances are your law-

yer will be terribly insensitive to your needs. That's when
you have a problem. Not only is he running up your bill, he
is delaying a transaction you desperately need resolved. The
answer? When you hire the attorney, demand, in writing, a
completion time table. Make sure this agreement states you
have the right to inspect your file at your convenience so you
can review what he is doing and when he is doing it. If your
lawyer objects, find a new lawyer.

    3. MOST GENERAL PRACTITIONERS IN THE LE-
GAL PROFESSION AREN'T VERY GOOD. They get along
because most people who hire an attorney don't really need
one, so any standard of performance is acceptable. That's the
way most lawyers work. They are adequate for standard legal work. They are pathetic on cases where professional performance is required.

    Why should you care? I hope you use a lawyer only
when it's truly necessary. If that's the case, when you do hire
an attorney you need results — which leaves the majority of
attorneys out of the picture. And that's another problem. In
many communities, especially smaller ones, all the lawyers
are incompetent. They're just GP's out to make a buck. But,
when expertise is called for they consistently lose. Or better
stated, their clients lose. You cannot afford to let this happen.

    Check on your lawyer. If he doesn't have a proven track
record on the type of case you bring to his office, find a
lawyer who does. Even good lawyers specialize, so this
record check is appropriate in all matters. Unfortunately
most of us run to "our" lawyer every time we have a problem.
I don't care how good your lawyer is, that approach is a mistake. You want a specialist with a proven, winning record.

    It should be noted that, if you are not satisfied with
your lawyer's answers about his record, don't allow him to
refer you to another lawyer. Why? Because, although you'll
never know this, most referrals include a fee or fee-splitting
agreement between the attorneys. That may mean you are
going to pay more. Find your own lawyer.

4. WATCH OUT FOR THE RETAINER. A straight retainer means you pay a fee for the lawyer agreeing to represent you. That's it, nothing more. When he actually does something he will charge you additionally. Most people never understand how a retainer works. It is kind of like the local grocery store demanding that you pay a large fee to walk in the front door, with groceries being extra. Would you shop there? Of course not. Yet, lawyers ask for, and routinely receive, large retainers for doing nothing. They get away with it because people are intimidated or don't understand.

If you are willing to pay a retainer, make sure it is a deductible one. That way future charges are assessed against what you already paid. For example, if you paid a $500.00 deductible retainer and the lawyer charges $50.00 per hour, you have 10 hours of work coming without further charge. If you have the standard retainer, those first 10 hours are going to be an extra charge.

As with all agreements, you need to hammer out your lawyer's representation to your satisfaction. And, get it in writing.

Never forget that your lawyer works for you. If you're not satisfied, fire him!

You cannot afford to let any attorney, even yours, get the upper hand in the client/lawyer relationship. This is especially true if your relationship falls apart. That's when your lawyer starts threatening to sue, withhold your files, etc. Of course, the best way not to have a problem with your lawyer is to take complete command from day one. Don't be afraid to ask questions. Don't be afraid to request fee schedules. Don't be afraid to negotiate the fee. Don't be afraid to ask for a written agreement. In truth, lawyers aren't the only ones to blame for lawyer rip-offs. The clients have to share a portion of the blame. After all, they're the ones who allow them to get away with it.

Remember, just because he or she has the word attorney in front of their name doesn't mean that they deserve your business. Demand the same standards from your attorney that you do your doctor, your garage mechanic, your banker, your grocer. In many cases, when you do, you'll find it's time to find a new attorney.

HOW TO SOLVE ATTORNEY BILLING DISPUTES

All financial relationships should be based on a written agreement. Such a preventive measure precludes many difficulties, since it's much easier to take precautions before the fact than to resolve disagreements later. Having a contract will save you aggravation and money.

That's not to imply that you should run to your lawyer to transact everyday business. That would be costly and foolish. For most transactions you don't need a lawyer. There are numerous legal form kits that are more than adequate to protect your position. Major transactions, however, demand review by an attorney, not necessarily because it's imperative, although it may be, but rather as a form of protection if mistakes are made. Having retained an attorney, you have the right to sue for malpractice if his error causes a loss. In those cases where you don't need a great deal of legal help, it is wise, if you're unsure, to have an attorney review what you've accomplished on your own. This strategy often provides the same results at half the cost.

The best way to keep the lawyer/client relationship in balance is to commit it to writing in the form of a contract. It's amazing how many attorneys, who correctly advise their clients to get other relationship/transactions in writing, ignore their own advice. The result? The client gets a huge unexpected bill he doesn't understand. With all the costs involved in a legal dispute, it makes sense to know what your lawyer is going to provide and at what price. Ask questions. How will you be billed? Will he be doing the work or will his staff? Are phone conversations charged to time? Does this include secretarial costs and at what price per hour? What about copy charges? The list, as you can see, is endless and varies with each case. That's why you must have a non-boilerplate written agreement.

As anyone who has failed to have an understandable contract with their lawyer can tell you, it is a critical issue. Thousands of people every year go to their attorney to resolve a difficulty and end up making matters worse. Their case never gets resolved to their satisfaction and a billing problem is created. Not surprisingly the attorney, because of the inherent unfairness of the relationship, usually wins these disputes because he can take you to court, at virtually no cost to him, while you have to hire another lawyer to fight his unreasonable charges. This happens frequently. That's why there are tens of thousands of attorney complaints filed with state bar associations every year.

Of course, the way to mitigate this possibility is to get the relationship in writing first. Dot every i and cross every t. If your attorney isn't a willing partner in this exercise in prudence, find another attorney.

Even when you take every precaution, disagreements can occasionally still occur. That's because our court system is designed by lawyers for lawyers. That truth notwithstanding, there are steps you can take if you contest your lawyer's bill.

1. NEGOTIATE. Contact your attorney in writing, explaining why you dispute the bill. Offer to settle for an amount you think fair. Does this work? One of my consulting clients, following my step-by-step counsel, negotiated his lawyer's bill from over $13,000.00 to $500.00.

2. FILE A MALPRACTICE SUIT. If your complaint with the bill is due to unprofessionalism, and you suffer a subsequent personal loss because of his error(s), you have malpractice recourse. However, malpractice cases are seldom won by clients because the deck is stacked; i.e., you have to find an attorney to sue a fellow lawyer, and then you have to plead your case in front of a judge who's a member of the legal fraternity. Even former Supreme Court Chief Justice Burger indicated that the closely knit brotherhood of lawyers works to the detriment of clients in this regard.

3. USE SMALL CLAIMS COURT. The only potential problem here is that the dollar limit set by some state small claims courts may be too small. However, if your dispute falls below the level of your state, this is a viable avenue. Additionally, if your state allows, you can save money by

representing yourself in small claims court, and may be able
to demand a jury trial, which can generate a helpful sympathy the lawyer will be unable to match.

4. FEE ARBITRATION. Almost all state bar associations have established a fee arbitration program in response
to the hugh volume of client complaints. Under normal circumstances, and assuming direct negotiation didn't work, it
is the best option. The advantage of arbitration is that it's
free (or inexpensive) and fast. More importantly, over half
the states have arbitration panels that are staffed by attorneys and a representative number of non-lawyers, which
helps ensure a modicum of impartiality.

An attorney fee dispute is a two-way street, meaning
the lawyer may be suing you to collect his unreasonable fee
while you are trying to have the fee lowered or waived. Arbitration, therefore, can save you the potential hassle and expense of being sued.

Arbitration panels usually require that you and the
lawyer agree to abide by its decision — a reasonable request
in light of the effort they undertake. Knowing arbitration is
available should encourage everyone not to pay an uncon-
scionable attorney bill. In many cases, once a lawyer is
served with an arbitration notice, the attorney will immediately try and negotiate directly with the former client —
which is what should have been done in the first place. However, because lawyers know the odds are in their favor, they
don't rectify matters until they realize they have a client
who fights back.

To locate the fee arbitration panel nearest you, call your
state's bar association (they're in the phone book) and ask
the following:

1. HOW FORMAL ARE THE HEARINGS? Formality
indicates seriousness. A casual hearing may mean the panel
is serving as nothing more than a shill for the lawyer's protection while giving the appearance of consumer interest.

2. HOW IS THE PANEL STRUCTURED? Is it staffed by lawyers, non-lawyers, or a combination? Watch out if your case will be presented to another lawyer's office for resolution. This reflects cronyism and almost ensures your legitimate grievance will not receive a fair hearing.

3. IS THE ARBITRATION BINDING? Why bother if it's not?

4. WILL THE ARBITRATION PANEL ASSIST IF THE LAWYER IS UNCOOPERATIVE? In some states, if the attorney refuses to submit to arbitration, the panel will pay for you to be represented if the matter goes to court.

As you can tell from the above questions, panels vary greatly from state to state. Some are good, some aren't. Some are truly interested in fairness, others are a facade to give the appearance of fairness. You have to know which your state offers. Arbitration by the former offers promise. The latter is a losing proposition.

In addition to the questions, ask if they have a brochure outlining their procedures. If so, follow their guidelines to the letter, as that makes a good impression with the arbitrators.

The general arbitration scenario is, you will be asked to file a complete written explanation of your dispute. Available documentation will be requested. After reviewing the evidence, the panel may make a decision without going into a hearing, but that's unusual. If a hearing is required, you and the attorney in question will receive notice as to date, time, and location. While an arbitration hearing is not a court of law, I cannot stress enough that being prepared may be the difference between winning and losing. This adage applies: failing to prepare is like preparing to fail. Upon reviewing the hearing evidence and testimony, the panel will notify you and the attorney of its finding.

The system available to the public for attorney fee disputes is, in too many states, so skewed in the favor of the attorney that it gives cause to believe the best thing to do is pay the bill and forget it. I look at it another way. Yes, chances are you'll be at a disadvantage, but, if you believe the bill is padded and/or you're not satisfied with his effort, you have no alternative but to protect your interests. It won't be easy. There's only one thing worse — paying the bill without a fight.

CONTACTING THE AUTHOR

To reach me with any comments, questions, or consulting needs, write: Reliance Enterprises, Inc., Post Office Box 413, Marengo, IL 60152.

Finally, I would like to respectfully recommend that you consider a subscription to my newsletter. *MONEY INSIDER* is dedicated to giving you the confidential information your stockbroker, banker, lawyer, and others don't want you to have. I know you'll be pleased with the uniqueness of your format, the value of our market counsel, and the immediate benefit of each article.

If you would like to review a free issue, send a business size SASE and $3.00 for handling to Reliance at the above address. To subscribe, send $49.00 for twelve monthly issues to: *MONEY INSIDER*, 1206 Alsace Way, Lafayette, CO 80303-0070.

About the Author

Edward F. Mrkvicka Jr. (pronounced mer-vick-a) rose from being a bank teller to CEO and president of a national bank in Illinois in just seven years . . . and then left banking after six years in power because, "I've always been consumer oriented and have felt obligated to make my knowledge available to you, so you can make intelligent financial decisions — decisions that will save you tens of thousands of dollars."

He is a registered investment adviser with the Securities and Exchange Commission, a member of the advisory council of the American Monetary Foundation, and a certified international financier. He has been published in the Chicago Tribune, the Chicago Sun Times. Boardroom Reports, Bottom Line Personal, Financial News Analysis, The Treasury Monetarist, Venture Capital News and many more . . . as well as featured in the New York Daily News, the Boston Globe, USA Today, Consumer's Digest, Syvia Porter's Active Retirement Newsletter, Family Circle, and over 400 radio and television stations.

He has been named to Who's Who of Emerging Leaders of America, Men of Achievement, and has been awarded the American Biographical Leadership Award for "Extraordinary Achievement in Banking and Finance."

NOTES

NOTES

NOTES

NOTES

NOTES

NOTES

NOTES

NOTES

NOTES